BROKEN

BROKEN

A MEMOIR

LEON R. WALKER JR.

Columbus, Ohio

BROKEN: A MEMOIR

Published by Gatekeeper Press
2167 Stringtown Rd, Suite 109
Columbus, OH 43123
www.GatekeeperPress.com

ISBN: 9781642370355
ISBN (Hardcover): 9781642370683
eISBN: 9781642370690

Printed in the United States of America

Dedication

THIS BOOK IS dedicated to my parents, Leon Robert Walker Sr. and Sylvia E. Gaither. Although I never told you, I really appreciate the hard times. They had an everlasting effect on me. Because of the unplanned setbacks, struggles, and lonely nights, and how you managed them, I have grown into a grateful man. Thanks to the harsh times, fear, uncertainty, and confusion that we endured, I am now more empathetic toward all human beings. Directly and indirectly, you developed me into a servant, and I owe you my life for it, as I have been able to share that special trait with others.

Watching your tumultuous marriage, I learned to fear commitment, but I also remember the good times that you shared, and it made me want to love and be married, like no other. I wanted to emulate your caring ways, and I wanted to love like the two of you loved each other when times were good—and bad. For that, I will always cherish those memories.

You raised strong, confident, and loving children. You worked hard to protect us. You gave us what you didn't have while growing up, and in many ways, we were able to duplicate your outgoing personalities, loyalty, kind hearts, and kindred spirits. Even now that you're gone, I am still able to love you, honor you, and respect you as if your bodies were here on earth, only because I feel your spirits each and every day. I salute you.

My brother Ralph, you came into my life at the right time. I needed everything you gave and taught me, each and every ounce of love and respect. My brother Donnie, thank you for the guidance during our tough childhood. You took on a lot, taught me a lot, and stood the test of time. To my sister, Toni, we've shared a lot, gone through a lot, and endured a lot. You are, and have always been, my best friend, the greatest sister anyone could ask for.

Love you all to life!

Contents

Acknowledgments

To my children, Kayla, Kamarin, and Aamir, you're the reason that I live, breathe, love, work, inspire, aspire, and seek to be God's greatest creation. Even though I have been tough on you, strong for you, and weak during trying times, I never lost focus on being your dad and father. There is a difference.

To Renee, Mrs. Coker, Mr. Coker, and Lance, thank you all for accepting me and my flaws from the beginning. I know it wasn't easy, but I do appreciate it from the bottom of my heart.

Outside of that, the hard work of writing my book and everything that's gone into it rests squarely on my editor, book mentors, and cover designers, who have helped me in many ways to bring my story to life. Thank you to Dr. Alice Vitiello, Roger Gogan (retired Navy Chief) Harold Nance (retired Navy Chief), John Sheppard, Nancy Manning, Bryant Martinez, and Rebecacovers.

Alice, you're an amazing person. I really appreciate all your help, guidance, sage counsel, wisdom, and advice. From your editing, I have earned not only how to become a better writer, but my grammar has improved immensely. After you told me that you knew how to box, I knew to be careful with our dialogue—either over the phone or in person—as I didn't want to get you upset and then have to face you. Needless to say, I did whatever you suggested, even though you always asked me if I was okay with any changes. In addition, after I watched a video of one of your fights, I felt bad for your opponent, which made me feel as if I didn't want to be in the ring with you. I'm happy you and I don't have to spar, as it could be quite embarrassing for me. You brought my book to life just as you inspire your kids and coworkers. Thank you very much. I salute you.

Roger Gogan, thank you very much for accepting my friend request on Facebook. Although it had been years since we spoke, you still remembered that the Chief's Mess got you and your family into the Khaki Ball that year. I believe it was 2009 or 2010 when you wanted to attend but didn't have a ticket. We got you and your wife in that night, and also provided daycare for your kids. That's what the Chief's Mess is all about: taking care of our fellow sailors and their families. You have since instructed me on how, when, and what to write, and you gave me the invaluable advice to take my time. Your instruction, wisdom, and guidance have not only kept me on a narrow path, but have also made writing extremely fun. Meeting you for coffee was fun as well, especially the second time when you asked me to meet you in the local library. I had been in the Illinois area since 2000, and didn't even know there was a library in the Gurnee area. Thank you for that introduction. You taught me about publishing, printing, how to get an ISBN, locating the Library of Congress, and many more things that will help any aspiring author. For all that, I salute you.

Harold Nance, a.k.a. "the chief" and my fellow chief, my buddy, my close friend: you are an amazing man. You're very talented, loyal, and one of the most passionate men I have ever met, and I've met thousands of people. The young sailors in your barracks at Naval Station Great Lakes (the 250 of them that you led for three years), as well as those that you led on the aircraft carrier, all still have great things to say about you.

I remember when we first met that you couldn't—or didn't want to—do many push-ups after running and completing the rest of the exercises. During your transition year to chief, you took it upon yourself to work on that, and you ultimately became stronger. What made me proud of you wasn't that you wanted to do better at physical training, but that you had become mentally stronger—overnight, it seemed—and I witnessed that with my own eyes. Keep that mental strength.

Thank you for doing my retirement program. And I also want to thank you for doing my book cover, although it changed many times, you initiated the process. That night back in June of 2016, I texted you with my vision about the book cover, and within a few minutes, you e-mailed me a very *hot* product. Thank you, my friend, for being extremely talented. I would also like to thank your parents for allowing me to serve with you.

John Sheppard, what a great author you are. During the years that I have known you, I could tell that you were a very cerebral man. Your work with the naval base newspaper was always impressive, but your methodical approach, wit, and uncanny ability to communicate so smoothly let me know that there was something special about you. Sadly, it took me a few years to figure it out, mainly because I had never been an avid reader. Today I know that you are a great author, and it all makes sense now. Thank you for your guidance, direction, and advice. I have taken it all on board.

Nancy Manning, you are truly wonderful. You helped me every step of the way. Even when I was tired or didn't want to talk about the book—didn't even want to reread it—you stayed on me about my vision and purpose. You kept me motivated, on track, and engaged. Although there were times that I didn't want to talk, you found a way to get me to talk. You are by far one of the most inspiring, determined, dedicated, wise, and intelligent women I've ever met. You helped me bring my book to life, and for that, I will forever be indebted to you. As amazing as you are, you continue to give, and you give unconditionally, which few people do today. I must say, I am extremely happy to have been able to share this with you, to receive your blessings, and to benefit from your advice and encouragement. Thank God! And thank *you* very much.

Mr. William Greenleaf: wow, where do I start? First off, I am grateful and thankful that using Google, I found your website and also found you on Facebook. It wasn't luck. Finding you, meeting you, speaking to you, and taking in your guidance for my book was meant to happen. It was destiny. You have taught me a lot about writing. You made it extremely easy. You were fair, up-front, and you were honest. I must admit, after reading your credentials, I was afraid to send you my manuscript. You have been reading and writing for many years, and I didn't think that my book would appeal to you. I was wrong. Thank you again for helping me turn my life into a book that, to my way of thinking, lots of people will read and enjoy, and that will inspire them to grow as well.

Bryant Martinez. You delivered the final book cover. Like I mentioned earlier in this acknowledgement, it changed many times, but because of you, we came to the conclusion of a very solid product that makes my story even more appealing. I know it took a while, and during those times, we simply grew patient. Once you completed my book cover, you were just as happy as I was, and that made me extremely grateful for your talent. You are an amazing artist, one that will surely go far. When I saw the picture you drew, honestly, I could not believe how closely it resembled me. You have a gift from God, and you blessed me with your talent, and for that, I am honored to acknowledge you in my book.

Rebecca covers. I searched and found you, by trial and error. It was well over a year ago, maybe longer, when I needed that gratifying, final touch, that intense focus, that driven work ethic to take my book cover over the top, and you did it, each and every time. You are an amazing person, and designer, thank you very much.

Preface

FOR THOSE CHILDREN who are struggling with life each and every day, I was you. For those of you who are being broken, damaged, abused, left alone, and given away, I was you. Here I stand before you to tell you my story. I'm going to discuss a way of life that most people know nothing about, but all of you who have been through it or are going through it now will understand. See, like you, I have been broken down to my purest form, and as you will read, I remained wide open for many years. Still, I'm here to tell you today that there is hope. There was hope for me, and there is hope for you. That's what this book is about. This book isn't just about tragedy. It's a story of survival. I want you to know that you can and will survive. I'm living proof of that.

The events in this book took place between 1970 and 1983, a period that began more than forty years ago. That's a long time. But everything that happened to me, every challenge that I faced, is still happening today to youth and adults everywhere. These tragic times were unavoidable for me. Once you live through them, they'll stay with you forever. It's your choice to do something about them, though. I learned that the hard way. Hopefully, this book will make the process a little bit easier for you.

How did I survive? The will to make it through started deep within myself, down in my soul. What I learned is that God gives you what you need to survive. It's all within you, and you find it when you learn how to count on yourself. These struggles don't discriminate. Anyone is susceptible to the things I fell victim to. Abuse, violence, poverty—these things don't pick or choose whose lives they touch.

Just remember that whatever life has in store for you, whatever tragedy befalls you, you do have a choice and a voice in the matter. Choice is critical here. I couldn't control the bad things that happened to me as a kid, but I could control the choices I've made since then—and, luckily, I've made good ones. That's the only reason I'm still alive to tell my story.

I am not afraid of my truth anymore,
and I will not omit pieces of me to make anyone comfortable.
                                                    —*Anonymous*

PROLOGUE
I Hated Christmas

I T WAS CHRISTMAS at my grandparents' house. We were on the west side of Cleveland. The year was 1972. The house was well lit outside with beautiful colorful lights. A small flurry of snow adorned the windows. The streets were covered, and you could hear the wind blowing through the door.

My grandparents always erected a huge tree in the living room and placed wrapped gifts at the bottom of it. The house was fairly crowded but had just enough room to be comfortable. Each friend and relative brought food to share. Banter flowed, and Christmas carols blurted from the small speakers on the floor. You know, the normal things on a Christmas day.

We could feel the excitement and love in the air. Kids ran up and down the stairs, opening gifts, laughing, and being playful. I had just sat down with my mother in the living room, and I began to get hungry. I could smell turkey, chicken, macaroni and cheese, mashed potatoes, potato salad—all kinds of food, including delicious collard greens simmering and bubbling. Steam lightly billowed from a large pot, filling the house with the aroma of smoked ham hocks. That and the smell of baked goods filled the house like a low-hanging cloud—but there wasn't a cloud, just tantalizing aroma.

I sat across from my mother, mouth tightly closed, legs crossed at the ankles, hands clasped, nose wide open. Hungry as shit, I raised my eyebrows two to three times, real quick, and shifted my eyes to the right, gesturing to my mother to make a quick escape to the kitchen.

She rose from the couch. "Excuse me," she said politely as she passed a group of people smoking cigarettes and drinking beer. This made it easy for our quick trek to the grub, close by. She swooped by, grabbed my hand, and off we went to the kitchen. We could smell those good greens brewing, and we just had to have a small taste.

I looked up at her with a sheepish grin on my face, and she looked down at me. We were both excited and smiling about the large spoon of greens we were about to devour.

My mother knew that I loved greens, and she loved them, too. All she wanted to do that day was to make me happy. "Doubleo," she said, "peep around the corner to make sure Mama isn't looking."

"Mama" was my grandmother, so I took a peep. Grandma wasn't anywhere to be found. "I don't see Grandma, Mommy."

"Okay," she said, "let's taste the greens."

"Cool," I responded with childish energy, swinging my hips from side to side like Chubby Checker doing the twist, delighted at my little treat.

My mother dipped the spoon in the large, simmering pot. Careful not to burn me with the hot juice now balancing in the spoon, she bent down and gave me my small portion.

I took a deep slurp of the hot juices and then moved my head to the side. "Mommy, these are very good," I informed her, my voice amping up.

"Be quiet, little boy," she said, grinning at me. "We're gonna get caught."

I inhaled the collard greens quickly, a grin on my face, eyes closed tightly, and my little head and miniature Afro tilted back. It was like heaven.

"Open your eyes, boy," she said.

I opened them, and we looked at each other as if we were being sneaky. We were. We both chuckled silently, though it was hard for me with my mouth stuffed. I was happy.

"Shhh," my mom said. "We're not supposed to be in here."

I put my index finger in front of my mouth to signal her to shush, too. Eyes wide open, wanting to burst into laughter, I covered my mouth with my hand, and we laughed again.

As my mom took the spoon up to her mouth to eat her small portion, in came my grandmother. I became stiff as a board because I knew this situation was about to get violent.

"What did I tell you, Sylvia?" my grandmother barked.

"What are you talking about?" came my mother's reply.

"Get the fuck out of my kitchen," Grandma snapped.

"Mama, don't yell at me," my mother said.

Out of nowhere, my grandmother slapped the shit out of my mother, right in front of me while I was still standing there holding on to her hand. The slap was so loud, hate filled, and thunderous, I thought Grandma had punched my mother. I was stunned and frightened, my legs jittery. My heart dropped immediately.

My mother stood there in amazement, staring into my grandmother's eyes. Her left jaw was getting darker and darker red with each passing second, and swelling at a fast pace, but she didn't move an inch. Everyone in the other room had heard the slap, and they ran to see what had happened. Meanwhile, along with the pee running down my leg, I could feel the tremors going through my mother's body, as if my grandmother had slapped me.

My mother's grip on my hand tightened. She wasn't going to let me go, even after being slapped. Had my mother fallen, I would have fallen with her. Had she crawled out of that house in pain, I would have crawled with her, willingly.

My cousin Joy zoomed into the kitchen. "Dorothy," she yelled, "why did you slap Sylvia like that?"

Crack. My grandmother slapped the hell out of Joy, too. She pointed her finger closely in Joy's face, waving it up and down, her head tilted, her other hand resting on her hip. "Listen, you stay out of it, bitch. That's my daughter, and if you don't like it, get the hell out of my house."

"Okay, Grandma," Joy replied, head down, holding her jaw. She left the house, fast.

My mother never raised her voice that day. She didn't even move. I felt horrible. I couldn't protect my mother from her mother. All I could do was look up at my mother, eyes full of tears, and say, "I'm sorry." I put my head down.

To see and feel my mother get struck like that by her own mother really shook me to the core. As I put my head down, tears dropped onto my little PRO-Keds shoes, my nose started running, and I didn't know whether to be angry with my grandmother or to still love her. I surely didn't like her slapping the shit out of my mother that day, over some damn greens. It had to be more than that. My mother's face was cherry red from the slap, and it was hard for me to look at her puffy red jaw.

"Why didn't you hit Grandma back?" I asked a few moments later.

"Well, you don't hit women," my mother explained. "You just don't do it, even if it's your own mother."

That day, and from then on out, my mother taught me a

couple things. One, she was extremely strong, and two, you never hit women, a valuable lesson for me at such a young age. I received that lesson, but the words exchanged that day stuck with me. To me, verbal abuse wasn't as bad as physical abuse. Physical abuse scared me while verbal abuse seemed funny to me. I would for sure learn the difference between the two later in life. They were both extremely hurtful, but I chose one over the other when I became upset.

Christmas was ruined, and ruined quite often. I saw abuse early on, up close and personal, and I never forgot it. I grew numb to it. Even when I learned how to abuse someone else—verbally or physically—I was numb to how they felt. I didn't consider the effects of abuse, mainly verbal abuse, either. The "I don't give a shit how you feel" attitude entered my soul very early. My words had become poison.

And through the years, my mother and grandmother were known to have extremely violent fistfights in the street.

CHAPTER 1

Good Roots

Little things matter.
Learn and know the matter in little things.

EAST CLEVELAND, OHIO, and Hough Avenue are my roots. I am not only deeply attached to my city, but I am forever grateful for Cleveland and the people who live there. Clevelanders especially love their athletes and their military. It's one of the few cities left that still really cares about both, and I'm grateful for that—grateful enough to mention it. It was here that I spent my childhood, and it was here that my demons planted themselves deeply in my soul.

I was between the ages of five and nine years old when the initial tragic events took place from 1970 to 1974.

My family had moved to East Cleveland from the inner city of Cleveland. Before moving to East Cleveland, we were living off Superior Avenue somewhere. I believe it was a street called Moulton. Prior to that, my father had lived on the west side of Cleveland, where he grew up. That was where he met my mother. In the early '60s, my father spent years in the violent Hough neighborhood located on the worst side of town in Cleveland. This is where it all began, really.

In 1966, there was a major race riot in Hough. Prior to the riots, there were about twelve thousand whites living there. It was upscale and a nice place to live, even having good Catholic schools. By the 1990s and early 2000s, however, you would never have known it to have been such a nice place. Life either forced the whites to move out, or it forced us blacks into poverty. The latter is really what happened. The truth of the matter is that whites and blacks have been trading places for years, but I feel that we as blacks were doomed from birth because of the color of our skin.

As blacks moved into the Hough area, whites moved out and into different neighborhoods. I say different, because Hough was still considered a good enough area to live in and raise kids until the demographics changed and it became known as a poor black neighborhood. Today, it has shifted once again. Poor blacks have moved out, and rich whites and blacks are moving back in. Talk about divide and conquer at its best.

Growing up there, we knew nothing different. We enjoyed what we had and thought that what we had was good enough—a lesson that I will return to in a bit. The important thing to remember is that thinking what we had was good enough became our mind-set, even though we knew deep down inside that we were better.

The things that I'm telling you now aren't just true about me. They're true about everyone who lived in Hough in those days. If you want to know why we are the way we are as blacks, I'll tell you. It might hurt to hear it, but I'm going to be brutally honest. It's because of coming from nothing and living in broken and dysfunctional households with divorce, murder, lack of standards, lack of organization, lack of morals, no insight, no guidance, no direction, and no caring. Worse yet, we get stuck. Once we achieve something, we either don't value it at all, or we value it so much that we forget where we came from.

You'll notice that I say "black" and not the more politically correct "African American." In fact, most of us actually prefer to be called black. It's a term that we grew up with. We also called each other "nigga," a term of endearment shared among blacks. "What's up, nigga?" we would say.

I never really understood that there were other black identities besides my own. I never knew much about people in Africa beyond the little bit that I learned in grade school, so it came almost as a surprise to me later in life when I learned that other people felt differently. I learned then that we as blacks are not accepted by the real Africans. They believe that we have been, and will always be, slaves of our own country. They see us as having been tainted by white America, so we are not their brothers, nor are our black women their sisters.

I was actually told this by an African man I met later in life. What was funny to me was that this African guy was in town to control a lucrative prostitution organization that included many Ethiopian women. He thought that I was tainted, but there he was, exploiting his African queens by way of the American crime of prostitution. Our conversation didn't last very long after I pointed that out to him.

Still, not everyone thinks this way. I was later fortunate to meet other African men and women who made it clear to me that they did not share his beliefs. Hearing this made me feel a lot better about what I was told early on. I started to read more about the continent of Africa and its history, just to educate myself about where my ancestors were from and what they had endured. It broke my heart to learn these things, but now I know.

On another topic, I believe that many blacks are very materialistic, though that isn't only true for blacks. We idolize sports figures, drug dealers, pimps, and hustlers. Over the years, as I sat down and thought about how materialistic we are, I realized it was what I was, and I was a part of it. I had become shallow, just like the others.

While I grew up around a strong circle of family and friends, I notice looking back on it that my priorities were screwed up. Although my parents made sure we went to school, did well, and respected our teachers, we weren't taught to value higher education at all. Was it because my grandparents didn't have an education, so there was nothing to pass down to my parents? Both of my parents dropped out of high school in the tenth grade. Conversation with family and friends in my household centered mostly around athleticism, wit, who gave the best parties, who had the best fighting skills, and who had the biggest penis—hardly academic topics. To this day, those topics of conversation haven't changed much among many blacks. This has been proven over and over again.

While over the years, blacks have gotten much better at valuing things that matter and teaching their kids well, there is still a ways to go. We are more aware now of the minimizing and dehumanizing stereotypes that are still prevalent today, but they come back to hurt us time and again because some of us continue to value the wrong things.

However, this isn't true for everybody. There are plenty of black families who expose their children to mentorship, guidance, and constant supervision, teaching them about the finer things in life. Part of this includes exposing them to people from other cultures, taking time to engage also with whites, Hispanics, Asians, and other ethnic groups. This kind of enrichment pays off. The blacks I know who were afforded the opportunity to branch out, or those who decided to do something with their life, have enjoyed stellar military careers and have become great leaders of the world. They also became solid pillars in the community, better-educated athletes, and have held down some of the most distinguished, lucrative positions in America, along with maintaining their athletic abilities.

I have found that it can be done: you can be an educated black man or black woman and still enjoy your athletic abilities, attend the prestigious universities, and do well in society. The negative stereotypes about blacks are only true about you if you live a life that makes them true.

One thing's for sure, and I will carry this for the rest of my life. A hidden source of mentorship and guidance for us young kids growing up on Alder Avenue in East Cleveland and on Hough Avenue, in one of the roughest parts of Ohio, was found in the older men and women in our neighborhood. Some were older than our parents, and some much younger but older than we were. I'm talking about the older cats and ladies in the neighborhood, the East Cleveland pioneers. They really cared for us, and I feel proud when I think back on this memory. I will cherish it forever.

All the kids that I grew up with, my siblings and myself included, were lucky to have had them in our lives. I have no idea who taught and led them, but they passed their knowledge down to us each and every day. Because of them, we were all great athletes. We had manners, we had respect for our elders, we attended school, and we also possessed a great work ethic. Believe it or not—and a lot of people don't know this—as young black kids, aside from the stereotypical basketball and football, we also learned how to ice skate, play tennis, swim, and wrestle—sports mostly thought of as things that white kids did, but we were all just as good, all because of the older cats in the hood.

For instance, I know that blacks have been playing golf for years. It just didn't get any attention until Tiger Woods came on the scene. We all knew about it, and the older guys were talking about it back in the '70s. There were even black lifeguards at the swimming pool back then. We all were Boy Scouts and Girl Scouts, too. I sure miss those days. We didn't realize that we were learning life lessons at the time. We just went along with it. But it really did help us. Not only did these experiences shape who I am today, but the lessons I learned back then would be my guiding light for years.

East Cleveland has had, and still has, some of the best athletes, musicians, and mentally strong people in the world. Our community was very tight-knit. Each time I go home, I make it a habit to look for these strong, positive men and women who led us. It really depends on what you are exposed to when it comes to what you know, how you think, and where you ultimately end up in life, and we were blessed early on to be raised the right way. I owe them my life, and they know who they are.

The white kids who grew up with us in East Cleveland were the same way. They shared the same mentorship that we did. We were similar to them in some ways—back then, they were even treated the way that we were when they committed crimes. Still, even though we shared a neighborhood and friends while living on Hough, those whites who interacted with blacks were still known as "nigger lovers." The white men loved black women, but wouldn't dare tell anyone, and the black women loved white men, but they kept this secret, too.

Despite being invited to our neighborhood, white people who didn't live there would never come. Instead, we would seek them out, because we were just as curious about them as they were about us. As you will learn later in this book, my life, at times, was a whirlwind when it came to race, creed, and ethnic groups, but it was all for the better. As I mentioned earlier, I grew up in Cleveland and East Cleveland. My family hadn't traveled that much, and aside from blacks and whites, Cleveland wasn't a terribly diverse city at the time. As a result,

I didn't grow up with much experience with Mexicans, Puerto Ricans, Filipinos, Indians, Russians, Chinese, Koreans, and people of other races that I've gotten to know later in life. Because my upbringing was somewhat sheltered in this regard, I became extremely curious as to what it would be like leaving Cleveland and learning about the other cultures. Either good or bad, I wanted to know what the world was like as far as people were concerned. Much later in life, I would find out.

As I mentioned earlier about whites in our community, they were on the same social ladder as we were, so as strange as this may sound to some, they were considered just as black as we were. They smoked Newports and weed, drank the same gin, and even spoke like us. Even now, for the most part, when you hear a white guy speak, if he speaks a certain way, you can tell that he spent time around blacks while growing up. This is true for white women, too. The crazy part is that the white women who grew up around us were more like black girls: curvy, with bigger booties, thicker thighs, and great dancing ability. Sometimes their families would disown them when they became "tainted" or started to like black guys, but we enjoyed every minute of it.

Blacks who grew up around whites were influenced, as well, for better and for worse. Most of them put more of an effort into education, but they also weren't great dancers, and they used entirely different recreational drugs. The white party culture was totally different from our own, and it was our white friends who introduced us to PCP, meth, cocaine, Marlboros, Camels, Winstons, ice, ludes, and acid. It shouldn't be a black-and-white thing, but in a way it is, simply because we grew up differently, so we are different but can share our life experiences, ideas, and lessons alike.

To the best of my knowledge, I distinctly remember only four white families in my neighborhood in East Cleveland. To this day, because of their presence, I have never had a racist bone, thought, or feeling in my body. I am extremely grateful for that.

My great-grandfather was white, as told to me by my grandmother. She said he looked like Abraham Lincoln: tall, skinny, and with a long beard. From my upbringing alone, I knew then that racism never had a place in my family, heart, or DNA, and I am very thankful for that.

No matter your social status or how powerful you feel you are, we are all equal. We came here by birth, and will leave in death.

CHAPTER 2
Messy, Lovable Creation

I HAD NOTHING TO do with how my grandparents met, why they met, where they met, or what forces brought them together, but I would surely pay for their encounter. You must be aware of your own family lineage and pedigree. As a kid, I knew nothing about this, and it would be the beginning of hell throughout my life. Don't get me wrong. My grandparents had a lot of great qualities, but I feel that the bad outweighed the good, and it was proven.

My mother and grandmother had, by far, the most toxic, dysfunctional relationship that a mother and daughter could have. Because of this relationship that I observed, I grew up with absolutely no idea how to treat a lady. My grandmother was known to be a great dresser and dancer. How could someone with such cool qualities become so abused and lose her self-esteem?

I guess she lost herself being in love with my grandfather and having children, as many women do—sad, but true. Even though she was verbally abused, my grandmother was very strong-willed, and she passed that quality down to my mother. She was tiny in stature—only five feet tall—but she was tough as anything. She drank a lot of beer, carried a billy club, and kept a gun in her purse.

Aggression was in my blood, and it came primarily from my mother's side of the family. Nevertheless, my grandmother was a great provider, and she was always very loving to us. That is, at least to the young men in our family—namely me, my brother, and my uncle, my grandmother's only son. I didn't find out until I was older that my grandmother and my mother never really liked each other. I'm not sure if that was DNA, learned behavior, or just pure hate, but whichever way, the demons manifested themselves throughout my entire family.

My grandmother was verbally abused in her household by her husband and son, who couldn't have been more than a teenager at the time. Before I understood how horrible this abuse was, growing up I would laugh at the despicable things that they called her: words like "dick," "ass," and "fucker." As I look back on it now, I realize that my grandmother was the only one verbally abused in that house. Years later, after speaking with my sister about my mother and grandmother's relationship, I realized why, in her anguish, she was so violent toward my mother, her only daughter.

My grandmother catered to my grandfather, my uncle, my brother, and me, regardless of how they spoke to her. That was how she was raised, I suppose.

Morning was brutal for my grandmother, and the disrespect didn't end there. It happened at every meal, with the same fierce, loud, thunderous cursing filling the house.

*　*　*

As I sat at the small, brown, crooked table, my back against the window, chewing a biscuit, a cigarette-filled ashtray in front of me, it was time to eat. I felt trapped, but my stomach was growling, and I was starving, so leaving the kitchen wasn't an option. As the grits boiled, and the bacon sizzled, I watched my grandfather's face and his piercing eyes.

He laughed at nothing, chuckled, and then smirked. "Dorothy, get your ass in here," he yelled, followed by a hard, shattering bang on the table.

With eyes no longer piercing but fixed on my grandfather, I did my best to eat, shaking in my chair, terrified. My mouth was full, but I was too afraid to even swallow. Granddad was smoking his long, thin Benson and Hedges cigarette, blowing smoke everywhere.

I said nothing, barely swallowing my food. I gave a slow, deep grunt, not wanting to annoy him any longer, and heard grandmother swiftly hustle into the kitchen, dodging through the heavy smoke, just to get what he wanted. Her short little legs thumping along in her bare feet on the kitchen floor, she quickly grabbed his favorite seasonings: hot sauce, salt, and pepper from the cabinet, and gently put them on the table. She didn't want the seasonings to make any noise. It was really sad to see that, but it seemed as if she was okay with it. His grouchy, frowned-up face ruled the scene and our emotions.

I knew better than to say anything as my food dropped into my stomach. *God*, I thought, *I don't want to be here anymore.*

His expression alone threatened that if she didn't do whatever he wanted, he would dismantle her.

Although there was fear, anger, arguing, and disrespect toward my grandmother, she still found time to take care of the men in the house. Aside from her wonderful cooking, she could bake her ass off, and she did it with passion. On many occasions, I could hear my little-bitty, wonderful grandmother in the kitchen shuffling dishes around. I knew then she was preparing to whip up a tasty meal.

* * *

Click, click, click, click. I could hear the large spoon whipping the cake batter in the bowl. I scurried into the kitchen and found my grandmother curled over the sink, one arm gripping a large white bowl, and her other hand twirling away. I couldn't wait to see what she was making. I stared at the bowl and blenders, feeling the heat from the stove. I knew then there was going to be a nice, hot, tasty cake coming soon. I was so excited and I couldn't wait for the cake to be done, so I asked, "Grandma, can I lick the spoon or blenders when you're done?"

"Sure, Doubleo. Just stand back for a minute, okay?"

I stood there listening to the blenders go at it. Then I heard the spoon whip the cake batter. I was perched on a kitchen chair, looking down into the deep bowl she'd filled with cake batter, eyes wide open, licking my crusty little lips.

She looked at me and said, "Once I pour the batter into the cake pan, the rest is yours."

"Just give me the batter, and I'll be okay."

We smiled.

"Okay, you can have a taste, little boy."

I licked the spoons clean, then the blender utensils, and then the bowl. "Grandma, this tastes really good," I said, rubbing my stomach.

We smiled again, and she winked at me. Soon, my sister would come in and I'd have to share either the bowl, the spoon, or the blender utensils with her. I didn't want to, but eating the cake batter with my sister and giggling like two little happy kids was pretty fun.

Not long after we'd eat the batter, and the cake and food was done, the onslaught of verbal abuse would come. These things were always done in front of my sister and me, and during these times, no one would dare say anything. Not that my mother condoned it, but when it happened, no one asked any questions. I guess my mother had seen this all of her life.

In my family, violence could happen at any time, and at any age. I hated what I witnessed, and it happened all the time. It still doesn't make sense to me. I witnessed verbal abuse quite often, which shaped the way I started talking down to women. My grandmother and mother had never been close, nor did they fix their volatile relationship, ever. It would have been nice to learn from both of them—they had so much to offer me as a little boy, and even as a young man—but it never happened.

* * *

My grandfather was known to carry a switchblade. He had roots in New York and Florida, which was probably why he was so prone to cut people. Not to mention, he was a measly five feet two inches tall with a bad attitude. His height, or lack thereof, had a lot to do with me being five feet nine, I believe.

He was a character. My memories of him are sometimes quite spooky, and at other times, fun. He played the drums in a band that performed around the Cleveland area and was known to slice people if things didn't go his way. His nickname was Blade. My grandfather was very good with his hands. He loved Cadillacs, smoking cigarettes, and had beautiful hair. He made most of the drums he played. He was also a collector of valuable coins. I never had a chance to meet anyone on his side of the family.

I do remember my grandfather and father having a great relationship, and when we did visit my grandparents, my grandfather would take us to get ice cream. But he wasn't a pleasant man to be with, and my sister and I were scared of him. He seemed to be grumpy all the time, possibly because he was ill—though we didn't know it—and that wasn't fun at all. He died on his job in 1982, and this would have devastating effects on my family a few years later, and for the rest of my life.

He had always kept one or two nice Cadillacs, and because of my grandfather, my uncle kept one, too. Even my brother received one when he was in high school. I found out later that before my grandfather died, he made it clear that when his grandchildren graduated from high school, they would each receive a Cadillac. My sister and I didn't receive anything when we graduated, and even my mother, who was my grandfather's favorite child, didn't receive anything after he died. Most likely we didn't receive anything because my grandmother and mother never got along.

CHAPTER 3

Gypsy Strong

When she transformed into a butterfly, the caterpillars spoke not of her beauty, but of her weirdness. They wanted her to change back into what she always had been. But . . . she had wings!

Mommy, I love and miss you very much. Thank you for continuing to fly. Regardless of the cards you were dealt, you always played your hand well.

*   —Your son, Leon Robert Walker Jr.*

MY MOTHER WAS a beautiful-looking lady, a well-known dancer, loving, and her zodiac sign was Capricorn. Like her mother, she was a great provider, but in the same vein, she also endured physical, mental, and verbal abuse at the hands of my father and other men. We'd always have great conversations, but some were shocking.

"Doubleo," my mom said softly one day, "never worry about what people say to you. Know who you are, do your best regardless of the situation, and you'll be fine."

"What do you mean?" I asked.

She took a deep breath, looked to her right, and slowly mumbled, as if ashamed, "He held me down. I yelled and screamed, but no one was there to help me."

"Who, Mommy? Who held you down?"

She sighed. "Well, I didn't want to tell you, but I was raped at an early age. Not just once, either."

"Huh? You mean he took sex from you? That's bad. Did he go to jail?"

"No, he didn't."

"Wait, wait. Did you tell on him?"

"No. He played baseball. He played professional baseball, and no one would have ever believed me."

"Well, what happened? Do you remember him?"

"Yes, I do. He was well-known, made a lot of money, and his team played against the Cleveland Indians, often right here in town. After the game was over, I wandered out of the stadium, accidentally bumped into a few players, and as I made my way down the street, there was a large crowd and plenty of noise. This one guy stood out. He was tall and thin and had smooth brown skin. He wore nice clothes, had a nice smile, with full lips and a thin mustache. 'Hey, pretty lady,' he said to me, 'How are you?'

"'I'm fine,' I said as we gazed into each other's eyes. Boy, was he nice-looking.

"We spoke for a bit. I knew he didn't have much time, so we sat at a park and just talked for a little while. It was dark out, and I could see him getting closer to me, so every time he moved closer, I would move away. Time went by. We played the move-over game for it seemed like hours. I guess by now he was irritated.

"'Well, I have to go now,' he said. 'We leave early tomorrow for another game in a different city, so I have to be ready to play.'

"'Okay,' I said. 'Nice meeting you.' As I gave him a hug, he grabbed me tight."

"Don't cry, Mommy. It's okay."

She cut me off. "No, no, he grabbed my neck, forced my mouth open, pulled my head back, and slammed me to the ground, forcing his tongue in my mouth. I was in so much pain, and scared. I didn't know what to do."

"What happened then? Please stop crying."

"He forced himself on top of me, tore my panties off, and spread my legs open with his legs. He raped me, and I bled a lot. He tore the rest of my clothes, covered my mouth, and just took sex from me. It's okay, Doubleo. Now don't you cry. We both have to be strong."

I cried with my mother. She wiped my tears. We hugged and just sat there quietly.

"I hate him, I hate him," I told her through my crying. "Why did he do that to you? I hate him."

"And I never got any help for it—no help at all. Later, I wouldn't be the type of person to want help or to get it, either."

I believe the rape my mother endured left her hopeless and feeling as if she didn't matter. I know for a fact she held it in and despised men for years to come. Some thought that she just wanted people to feel sorry for her, which couldn't have been further from the truth. My mother was tough, and now that I'm older, I know that I have some of her tough ways. My mother and I had a very close relationship and a unique bond. When famous athletes are accused of rape, the offender's image is often protected at the victim's expense. Who would have even believed that someone like my mother would have been in the company of such a well-known, high-paid athlete? It happens all the time, though.

Most women that it happens to are told that they put themselves in that predicament, which only causes the victim to feel hopeless, afraid, and always in danger. My mother had become closed off: she didn't seek relationships, and she saw her rapist's face in other men, so her downward spiral started long before my parents eventually divorced, and after they did, she didn't really want men around her children. She had lost total trust in most of them. While she was single, I can only remember one man being in my mother's life, and we weren't close to him at all. By the looks of him, I knew she wasn't into how good a man looked anymore.

* * *

"Hey, buddy, how are you? I'm Mr. Stinall."

"Hi, I'm Doubleo. Nice to meet you." I shook his hand, looked into his face, and saw two rotten brown teeth, gapped extremely wide. His purple-and-pink lips, slightly cracked in the corners, were crusty as hell. I knew he was a smoker. It damn near hurt to look into his eyes. His glasses were thick, and the slightly bent frames rode low on the bridge of his narrow brown nose. Nose hairs hung from his nose, and flickering from his ears were more hairs, black and gray. The hairs seemed to move when he spoke.

This dude is gross, I thought.

As we ended our handshake, he turned to walk into the kitchen. I could see that he was balding, the heels of his shoes were run over, and the top of his collar was dingy. His clothes were dirty, mismatched, and overall distasteful. He needed a haircut. A far cry from my father, but I suppose my mother saw something in him that my siblings and I didn't.

I'm glad he didn't talk much. His breath was horrible, so he did us a favor by keeping his mouth shut, or staying away. Had I been big enough, tall enough, I would have done my best to get his ass out of our house. I hated when he'd say something to me. He'd tilt his glasses as if he were intelligent, bend down, and start to talk.

Man, I thought, *say one more thing to me and my father will be over here to kick your ass.*

He also thought he was some type of therapist. I'd listen to him and my mom talk, and even though I was only twelve or thirteen, hearing some of the things he'd say, I'd think, *Will you just shut the hell up, brush your teeth, get a damn haircut, and leave.*

Some therapist he was. Far from it in my mind.

I was just used to my father. My mother's boyfriend wasn't around long anyway, and lucky for him. He had no idea who my mother could turn into. We would all soon find out. Her thoughts began to seem extreme, and I knew it was because of her rape. It's possible she held her being raped against my father. She also told me that since the well-known athlete was never charged, then she must have slept with him in a consensual way.

Despite all that had happened to her, she took care of the house, cooked often, took in other children, and made sure we had everything we wanted or needed. My mother would always dust, clean, and vacuum everything. She was extremely engaged within our household. We were spoiled and didn't have much money, but she made it work.

In East Cleveland, my mother redesigned our house on Alder Avenue, adding more color and lights inside. It was like a little disco. She knew some carpenters who built a stage in our house, a stage that my siblings and I would use for dancing, cartwheels, and even wrestling. That wasn't what it was for, but we did it anyway. My mother was also a den mother of Boy Scout Pack 336. She made chocolate chip cookies, homemade lemonade, pizza from scratch, and she taught us how to bob for apples and collect newspapers so that our Boy Scout troop could make money for the annual jamboree. My mother was a good manager of people and kids. She was very social, a great planner, nurturing, intelligent, and didn't take shit from anyone.

CHAPTER 4
Saddle Tramp

They call me a drifter, they say I'm no good
I'll never amount to a thing,
Well I may be a drifter and I may be no good
There's joy in this song that I sing . . .
I'm as free as the breeze and I ride where I please . . .
　　　　　　　　—"Saddle Tramp," Marty Robbins

I have endured, I have been broken, I have known
hardship, I have lost myself, but here I stand, still
moving forward, growing stronger each day.
I will never forget the harsh lessons in my life.
They made me stronger.
Daddy, thank you for showing us how to deal with
the struggles and be resilient,
for showing us both the way out and the way in.
Although you didn't mention the word love,
you showed us how to love through giving,
lessons, helping,
teaching, and guiding. I love you.

—*Your son, Leon Robert Walker Jr.*

A S A KID, my father was called "Saddle Tramp." He told me this when I was a teenager, and I never knew what it meant. Truthfully, I never even really cared until eighteen years after his death.

The words in the song are quite harsh in the beginning, but as you listen, it all comes together as to why they called him that. My father was six feet one or two, 230 pounds, a boxer, and he also played running back and cornerback for the army's traveling football team. He was dark-skinned, handsome, mean, tough, funny, witty, and caring, with broad shoulders—a very smart man with a huge heart. He loved to laugh and smile, and he possessed all natural muscles. Over his lifetime, he became a 33rd-degree Mason as well as a Black Nationalist, the latter movement being one that advocated for black separation from white society. He didn't hold these beliefs for his whole lifetime, though. Later in life, he changed his thinking, and concluded that it was wrong to separate us from whites.

My father was a foundry worker at Ford Motor Company for thirty-four years. When he wanted to, he grew a full beard. However, when he did so, he looked scary to me, very scary. He, too, had a wide mouth, but it came with a beautiful smile.

My father was a great provider. He took care of us and also other kids in the neighborhood. He loved trucks of any kind. He drank often. I suppose it was from the stress of working at Ford, and quite possibly, having three kids, but he still took care of us. He also received an honorable discharge from the army.

My father had two brothers and a sister. I never had the chance to meet his sister, who was killed in a car accident many years ago, probably before I was born. I did get to meet her son and stepson, an athlete who would later play linebacker for the Ohio State Buckeyes, and who was also drafted into the NFL to play for the Washington Redskins and Baltimore Colts.

I have two uncles on my father's side, one of whom was a boxer (a southpaw like me). He could roller-skate, fix cars, build go-karts, build minibikes, and he was a great provider to all of us. I loved it when he'd come over with my cousins. He'd always drive his camper. That was my favorite. He was a very intelligent man. You could ask him anything, and he'd have an answer. He also served time in the United States Army.

That uncle gave me my first go-kart, which changed my life. I had never owned such an exciting motorized vehicle, such an amazing sight to all the other kids in the ghetto. They all wanted to ride it, so I became a little entrepreneur early on, charging other kids to ride a couple of laps around the block. Just another way that I learned how to make money at such an early age and buy what I wanted to—specifically, candy for myself and the young ladies in my neighborhood.

My other uncle was good with us, too. A veteran of the United States Army, he loved to reminisce about his time there and to tell us funny stories. He had thick, fat fingers, always dark and greasy-looking, with swollen fingertips. His hands were scraped up and leathery, kind of like King Kong hands. They looked spooky. I suppose it was from his time in the army. His hands should have stayed in his pockets. I would soon find out what those hands would do when provoked, in more than one way.

He was short and had a wide mouth and a strong set of teeth. He smoked Lucky Strikes, probably the most powerful cigarettes on the market. He always complained about being broke, and he lived with us for years. I never understood that, but I always thought that he was cool to have around.

Although he was pretty cool, he did have a violent temper when his buttons were pushed. One day my cousin borrowed my uncle's car, and he stayed away for too long. After a while, my uncle got pissed about not having his car and my cousin being gone for so long. After many hours had passed, my cousin arrived with the car. As he walked up to our house, my uncle walked outside, and before my cousin could explain himself, *pow!* My uncle punched him in the jaw and knocked him out.

I was accustomed to hearing arguments and seeing violence in my family—at least on my mother's side—but this was on my father's side, and on one fateful night, the violence would erupt again. This time, both families would be involved, and it would involve both my mother and my uncle. More on that story later.

We mature with the damage,
not with the years.

I also have three siblings: two brothers and a sister. Growing up, my oldest brother and I were okay, but my sister and I were very tight. We're close in age—only eleven months and three days apart—and we shared a lot. We had a lot in common— both animal lovers, deeply involved in sports, busy with friends and kid parties, school activities, and family. Even though we loved each other, we fought often, and this might have been because we lived in an extremely violent household. Although we witnessed and experienced some great things in life, we also witnessed numerous tragic events that shaped who we are today. Neither one of us asked to be resilient, hard, tough, or stubborn, but it's in our DNA, so we had to manage it. We were literally a product of our environment, and it's still in our blood today.

My sister doesn't have any kids, nor has she ever been married. We were both affected by how we were raised, for better and for worse. My older brother has never married, and oddly, I have no idea if he has any kids—though I really doubt that he does. My other brother, Ralph, whom I didn't meet until 1979, has three kids, and he's from Alabama. I was fourteen when I first met him. In the middle of a family crisis, he came into my life at just the right time.

CHAPTER 5

Fist in My Mother's Mouth

**I heard the punch,
I lived with the results**

"B ITCH, I WILL kill you!"
These were the horrible words uttered from my uncle's mouth. I was only a small kid at the time. This was in the early 1970s, but I remember it distinctly, just as clearly as if it happened yesterday. The words, the scene, the pain . . . all of it remains.

We were at a party at my uncle's house. An argument broke out, and my mother obviously didn't like me being around all of these adults. She also didn't like whatever it was that my uncle had to say. I can still see them standing there in my aunt's bedroom. There was loud music playing—Marvin Gaye. People were drinking, dancing, eating, laughing, and having a great time. That would soon end.

The song that was playing would ring in my ears for years, not because of the lyrics, but because of what happened that night: "What's Going On," a very famous song that everyone loved, and I remember it like it was yesterday. I've learned as I've gotten older that songs can become anchored in your memory and tied to emotions—good things, bad things, tragic events—many things. This night was tragic, and so the song to this day still triggers my tragic memory of the night, even now as I write this book.

"Bitch, fuck you!" my uncle screamed. "I will kill you!"

The house was loud, full of smoke and people. Though it was packed, I could see their faces and the anger on both. I could see spit flying from their mouths. I stood a measly four feet tall or so, weighing maybe sixty to seventy pounds. What could I do? I was very short, so no one could see the tears streaming down my face.

We were in my uncle's bedroom. The lights were flickering, and it seemed as if his room was built for a horror scene. I looked up at the two of them. Trying to stop them, I yelled for my father as I could see the argument becoming extremely intense. Marvin Gaye's song blocked out my cry for help. No one could hear me. No one could even hear them arguing.

My left hand on my uncle's stomach, I tried to push him away as I kept my right hand braced against my mother's thigh. They were both furious, yelling, and I was pissing my pants. I could feel the pee running down my leg and into my shoes. My shoes were soaked with piss, and the floor was slippery as I continued to push the two of them back, but to no avail.

Suddenly, I felt my mother move away, and I saw my uncle turn from her. I thought everything was going to be okay, that I had succeeded in breaking them apart.

"Edward," my mother screamed, "don't call me a bitch. Wit yo short ass, you see my son standing right here?"

My uncle turned around and looked down at me. I closed my arms around my upper torso, hugged myself, took a deep breath, and stepped back. My uncle's fists were balled up tight, his bottom lip curled in.

I waited for him to slap the hell out of me, but he turned

back around. Immediately, I let out a heavy gasp, put my arm around my mother's waist, looked up at her, and cried out, "Mommy, don't yell, please."

"Move, Doubleo," she belted out. "I've had enough of his shit." My mother turned and grabbed a little portable TV from the dresser. It probably weighed about fifteen pounds.

My uncle turned back around to face her. His hands balled up, he approached her with a face full of fury, his mouth tightly closed, his eyes huge, spit still flowing from his mouth like a rabid dog. I could hear him say it again. "Fuck you, you bitch!"

Without hesitation, my mother lifted the small but heavy TV, and with all of her might, she threw it at him. I was standing right there, and I watched it hit him square in the face. Pieces of the TV flew everywhere. Blood sprayed on me, on my mother, and on the bed. The force of the blow knocked my uncle down. I started to scream and yell, not knowing who to be mad at. I was still hoping for my father to come back, but with the loud music, there was no way he could've known what was happening.

I tried to stop my uncle from getting up off the floor. He was angry like a pissed-off pit bull. I tried my best to stop him, but there was no way. As he was getting up from the floor, I was on top of him, his blood on my clothes, feeling his heartbeat through his clothes and mine. He was yelling at me to get the fuck off of him. I knew I was only a kid, and he knew it, too— just his small, frail, pissy, scared, and trembling nephew. He also knew from the blood all over both of us that his face was split open. However, there was no stopping him.

I remember the next part quite clearly: my uncle got up, full of rage, his fists clenched into balls. With all his might, he punched my mother directly in the mouth, knocking out two of her front teeth. I could hear the punch despite the loud music. It was like hearing a bat hitting a baseball from a powerful slugger with a full swing. With a loud crack, her head snapped back violently. I watched her teeth fly out of her mouth and land on the bed while she fell to the floor, hard and abrupt.

I tried to shield her as she lay there on the floor with my uncle standing over her. She looked up at my uncle and tried to speak through the blood filling her mouth, pain evident on her face. Blood squirted from her mouth, splashing on me. I could feel its warmth drip down my forehead and onto my face. I was crying, holding my mother tight as hell, and feeling her heartbeat through her clothes. My uncle still yelled as my mother fell quiet. I could feel her heartbeat while I was lying on top of her. She curled up on the floor, and I stayed with her. I could see my mother's face become disfigured right in front of me. Listening to her heartbeat slow, as if she was going to die, I held her mouth with my little hands and watched the blood dripping through them. Blood was everywhere. My tears fell from my face onto hers. We were both crying, our heartbeats in sync as she took deep breaths and so did I.

It all seemed like it was in slow motion. I was just a kid, and I didn't want my mother to die—not at any time, and especially not when I was holding her. I was terrified. My head was buried deeply in her chest, and I didn't want to let go. I didn't want to think of having to try and remove my hands from her mouth. The blow to her face and the violent snap of her head made me wonder how anyone, especially a man, could ever hit a woman like that. Her mouth was never the same after that powerful punch.

I looked up at my uncle. How I hated him. I wanted to kill him. He had hurt my mother, and he had hurt her bad. She would be hurt forever. As fearful as I was, I was not going to leave her lying there alone, so I waited for my uncle to leave the room. When he left, I crawled off my mother, slid across the floor in my pissy pants and onto the bed, where I saw her two front teeth on the blanket. As I reached to get her teeth, I trembled in fear, anger, and disbelief. With each stretch of my body to reach her broken teeth, I cried louder and louder. I extended my arms out to retrieve her teeth from the bed, but each time I tried, I pulled my hand back at the last minute, looking back to see if she was okay.

I didn't want to feel my mother's teeth in my hand. I didn't want to know for sure that they had really been knocked out. It's not supposed to be that way. And I couldn't stop looking around to make sure that my uncle wasn't coming back in. I finally found the courage to grab her broken, scattered teeth. It seemed as if I had been crawling on the bed for days.

"Come here," my mother mumbled through her broken mouth. "Let's go."

Her voice was shaking, and she could barely talk, but my mother was very courageous. I could tell that her pain was excruciating, but all the while, I knew that her mind was on the safety of her children.

Hearing her voice, I let out a deep sigh of relief that my uncle hadn't killed her. I was ready to go, but I didn't want to walk out of that room and face my uncle. I helped my mother get up. I could hear the ambulance outside. I knew that my uncle was hurt pretty bad, but I was happy that someone was there to take him away so that we could go home.

I couldn't understand why they had to hurt each other that night. How dare he do this to my mother, destroying her beautiful and precious teeth and face. I don't know where my father went that night. He had been at the party, but when the violent fight happened, he wasn't around—and that wasn't like him. He surely didn't ever say anything to my uncle about why he knocked my mother's teeth out, either.

That night was the first time I remember the hot, evil feeling coming over me, a feeling of wanting to kill someone. I hated my uncle for years after that and wanted to kill him for how he rearranged my mother's mouth and teeth.

When my mother and I came out of the bedroom, my uncle's wife cried at the sight of my mother's face. "Oh my God, baby, you need help," she said, handing her a towel.

My mother shook her head. "I'm okay," she mumbled through the cloth. "We'll just leave."

I knew at that moment just how strong my mother was.

We caught the bus home that night, my mother, my sister, and I—the #6 bus, to be exact. Her mouth swollen, her eyes full of tears, my mother stumbled as we walked to the bus stop. She held my hand, and I did my best to help her walk in the snow, my wet pants and all. We made it, but it was a nightmare. As we stood waiting for the bus, my pants started to freeze and get stiff. It was pure hell. My sister was quiet. She didn't know how to console my mother, and neither did I. All we could do was sit there together, waiting on the bus.

It seemed like ages—practically an hour—before the bus finally came. To get on the bus, my mother had to grab my hand and swing me up. My pants had frozen over, and I couldn't even move. To sit down was even worse. I remember thinking that if I could just pee my pants again, I could get warm and defrost them, but my piss was all gone from the fight that my mother had been in. As the bus headed down Euclid Avenue, we were shaking, my mother crying. Her mouth and towel were full of blood, and I held her tight, tears streaming down my face. I was trying to hold it in. Everyone on the bus was looking at us, but no one offered to help. I was embarrassed. It was a long, cold journey home.

We got home about an hour and a half later, and my mother lay down in her bed. My siblings and I could do nothing but look at her face in disgust, help change out the bloody towels, and cry through the night until we all fell asleep. The next day, my mother looked worse. She never did go see a doctor or a dentist for her injuries, but being out of that house where the party was and away from that chaos, we all felt safe, at least for the moment.

I wish I could say what happened to my mother was an isolated incident, but far from it. One night, I could hear my parents arguing. I got up off the floor in the bedroom I shared with my brother and headed downstairs. I could see my father on top of my mother, choking the hell out of her. He was looking down at her, dressed in his Ford Motor Company coveralls, straddling her midsection as she was stretched out on the couch. My father slapped and choked my mother several times. My mother tried her best to punch him, but she couldn't get up, nor would her arms reach him. She tried, time after time as I watched their altercation in fear. She squirmed left, then right. I could tell she was fighting for her life, her legs perched up on the end of the couch to help herself become free from his strong arms. When she moved one way, my father followed her, as if he was in sync with her desperate attempt to save her own life.

I wanted so badly to jump on my father's back and pull him off of my mother, but I was too small. All I could do was watch my mother struggle to breathe and yell at my father, "Daddy, please let Mommy go." My cries for help never calmed the situation. As I mentioned before, we grew up surrounded by violence at home.

Every year, as a family, we would travel to the west side of Cleveland to spend Christmas with our grandparents, and throughout the year, we visited them on weekends, birthdays, and other holidays. Don't get me wrong. My grandparents were pretty cool at times. But for the most part, I was scared to go over there. I knew that if there was going to be alcohol involved, then an argument, fight, abuse, or some form of unhappiness would shortly follow.

We got gifts on Christmas, and the Easter Bunny came yearly, but it seemed so lonely when my father didn't make that trip with us. However, when he did, it seemed for a brief moment like we were a normal family. My father would light up the room when he walked in and smiled. It was electric, and his smile was contagious. My mother and father would interact as if they were very happy. We all knew better and that this was only done in front of my grandparents, but for the time being, it felt good. It felt healthy. I finally felt for a moment like I had a normal family.

Upon returning from my grandparents' house each Sunday, though, we would always think about what would come next when arriving home. School the next day, parents arguing, a fight—there was always something, and not knowing what it would be didn't feel good at all.

CHAPTER 6
From Bullied to Bully

These were thrown into my face

**I could feel the evil and anger build every time
they stuck to my face**

I WAS NINE OR ten years old, it was summertime in 1974 or 1975, and we were back at Grandma's house on West 130th Street on the west side of Cleveland. The trees were full of leaves, bugs were rampant, and the day was clear. My uncle (my mother's brother) and my brother were like a team, and from what I can remember, they were evil at times—especially to me. One time, I remember them taking me outside to the backyard creek behind my grandmother's house, where the kids in our area used to play.

"Yo, Doubleo," my brother said. "Wanna go outside and play?"

"Sure, it's boring in here. Let's go."

As my brother and uncle headed outside, I joyfully followed them. To me, this was a time to bond with them and have fun. Little did I know, it wasn't going to be fun for me. I looked up to both of them and believed that I was in good hands.

Normally, when going into the backyard, it was to catch snakes and insects, and do whatever else we could get into back there: climbing on trees or the garage, or gathering twigs to make little boats and see whose boat floated the longest in the creek. It was pretty cool to build things with my brother, a really soothing time for us.

On the side of the house were big trees and ugly plants that carried what we called "cuckabugs." They were round, furry, about an inch in diameter, and covered with long, prickly spikes that hurt like hell when you touched them. Just touching one would cause excruciating pain, as all the kids who played back there knew.

"Turn your punk ass around," my uncle said.

"Huh, what do you mean?" I asked him hesitantly.

"You heard me, boy. Turn around."

As scared as I was, I turned around, and as I did, he threw the sharp, pointy, balled-up plants into my face. He did this time after time.

First, he was far away, about ten feet. "Be still," he yelled, "and don't move." He underhanded them into my face and head. "Does it hurt, punk?"

My brother, leaning against the tree, arms crossed, chuckled under his breath each time my uncle tossed one and it stuck to my face.

"Stay right there and don't move. I'm gonna get closer."

Tears streamed down my face. He tossed another one, and I tilted my head slightly, but I was too terrified to move. He missed, but by this time, he'd thrown about five or six, and each one stuck to my face.

"Oh, you think you're smart, huh? I told your ass, don't move. Okay, since you can't listen, I'm coming closer." My uncle came nearer.

I peeked to my left to see where my brother was. He was still leaning against the tree, chuckling even more now. I'm sure I looked like a little short clown with a face covered in fur, but far from the comfort of fur.

"Boy, I told you, don't move. Now, just for moving, I'm going to throw more at you." He moved closer, knelt down, and smashed a few more into my face. "Now, how does that feel?"

I cried and withered in pain, pissing my pants, but I stood still, in fear. "Why are you doing this? Why?"

My uncle just laughed hysterically, in a low tone, slightly covering his mouth, so as not to be heard and get caught.

My brother straightened up and walked over to me. "Damn, man, you're pretty messed up," he said.

My face felt warm, not from the heat outside, but from the blood streaming down it. "Can you take them out?" I asked my brother, through bouts of tears and deep breaths. "How bad are they? Am I gonna be okay?"

"Yeah, just go inside and pull them out of your face. But don't tell Mommy."

I went inside, my pants wet, my shoes soaked from the piss, and headed to the bathroom.

As I tried not to tell on them, my mother abruptly stopped me. "Oh my God," she said. "What the hell is this?"

"They threw these things into my face. It hurts, Mommy. It hurts bad."

"Come here, Doubleo," she said. "Sit down so I can take them out of your face."

My mother spent hours pulling those things out of my cheeks, forehead, lips, eyelids, chin, and earlobes, and then rubbing Vaseline on my face. I will never understand why my uncle and my brother did that to me that day, pelting me again and again in the face with those things. I was petrified. All I could do was stand there and take it. I hated what they did to me. To them, it was fun and games, but to me, it was pure hell and horror. I stood there crying, shaking, and writhing in pain, wetting my pants from the agony and terror while my uncle and brother just laughed and kept throwing those hurtful things into my face again and again. The more they threw into my face, the more I cried, and the more I peed my pants.

As I stood there shaking and peeing, they laughed louder and louder. I had no idea where my father was, but I knew that if he had been there, it would never have happened. I'm not sure how long this went on, but it seemed like forever. Even today, it's hard to think back and relive it. After a while, I just stood there and took it. This was the beginning of my toughness. It came in an uncomfortable way, but it came, and I would be changed forever because of it. Some kind of way, that strength to take pain like that entered my soul. I would later transfer that pain into other things—some very good, and some not so good—more like evil.

Yes, I was exposed to lots of violence growing up—that side of my family (my grandparents, uncle, brother, and mother) was very dysfunctional, with lots of weed, alcohol, arguing, hatred, and fighting. But it was this experience in my grandparents' backyard that became a turning point for me, and not for the better. It was the start of my anguish and of me wanting—

and liking—to be a bully. It was only the beginning of how I was transformed into what most people didn't know I was: a monster. It was due to experiences like this that behind my innocent face, small body, and quiet demeanor, there formed a scared, demonic, hateful being.

I learned how to be a bully, and the first person that I began to bully was my sister.

CHAPTER 7

The Violation

What's important to you?
What you are important to.

MY MOTHER'S SIDE of the family was totally dominated by men. By not experiencing women being treated right, or fairly, in my family, I became clueless as to how to treat women. The men in my family certainly didn't model that behavior for me. What I learned from them instead was how to mistreat women, a learned behavior at its "best." This became an ongoing theme in my life, which would rear its head again and again as I grew older.

It was 1971, and I was six years old and in the first grade. On a cold, wintery day, my parents had both gone to work, my siblings were gone, and I had overslept. My two female cousins and I were home alone.

I would be sexually assaulted for the first time in my life.

"Doubleo, come upstairs," my cousins yelled. "We have something to show you."

What was I to do aside from going up to see what they wanted? I quickly ran up the stairs and turned the corner. I leaned on my sister's bedpost, arms crossed, smiling and chewing gum. I loved gum and candy, and they'd always have some for me.

"Come here, cutie," my cousin said, slightly pinching my cheek. "Your front tooth is out." She pointed at it.

"Yep, came out last night, and the tooth fairy left me seventy-five cents." I shoved my hands into my pockets to show her my coins. "See? I want to go to Gus's candy store after school." I smiled from ear to ear. "Can you take me later?"

She never replied. I saw my other cousin sitting on the bed, quiet, staring at her sister out of the corner of her eye. I suspected something wasn't right. They had a weird look on their faces, but they were smiling, so I felt comfort come over me and smiled back.

These are my cousins, I thought. *They're much older than I am. I'm safe.*

My one cousin grabbed me and threw me on the bed, with a quick whip of my short little body. "Aha, got yo ass," she grunted. "Fuck some candy."

I was kicking and wiggling.

My other cousin got on top of me and started to cover my mouth with hers. "Girl, hold his damn legs," she said. "He's strong."

"Just get to his mouth," my other cousin replied. "Get to his mouth."

Her mouth remained over mine, rough and open. I felt suffocated at first, then I felt the pain from the swollen area of my missing tooth. It throbbed. They both took turns with me, even with blood slowly filling my mouth. They moved to my neck, my jaws, and my entire face.

At first I cried. Then fear came over me. I didn't want to upset them and have the scene turn violent. After all, they were older, taller, and much stronger than I was, so I submitted myself to them. This went on for the entire morning until they made me go to school. Our school was close to our home, maybe a mile or a little less, so yes, I walked to school that day, still shaken from the incident, but I tried my best to hold myself together.

As I entered Chambers Elementary School, my teacher, Mrs. Taylor, looked at me with horror in her eyes. She was a tall lady, with long black hair, a thin build, and a motherly figure. She always wore long skirts and nice shoes. I really liked Mrs. Taylor. She was one of the teachers who gave us candy if we did well on spelling test.

I had no idea how bad my face appeared until she grabbed me and looked at it closely. Her eyes wide open, she asked, "Are you okay? Look at your face!"

"Yes, I'm okay, Mrs. Taylor," I told her. "I had a fight on my way to school."

With that, she called my mother. My classmates laughed, and I knew then that I looked comical. It was funny but serious, all at the same time. This was my time to cry, and I did.

"Come here, young man," she said, and gave me a hug.

I ran into her arms as quickly as I could and held her tight for the entire morning. I had no one to hold me close and make me feel secure, so being in Mrs. Taylor's arms felt so good, so safe, and so comforting.

She slightly pulled my head away from her stomach. "Look at me," she said.

I raised my head to look up at her.

"Oh God, Leon, you're bleeding. Here, wipe your mouth."

What my cousins did to me that day pissed my mother off, but I'm not sure how, if at all, they were punished for it. Even after the incident, my cousins would still visit us often. The one cousin who kissed and sucked on my face and neck died years later, an alcoholic in her early fifties, and my other cousin was brutally killed by her boyfriend. When her body was found stiff, in a field on the rough side of Cleveland, the knife he used to carve her up was still buried deep inside her. She was only in her thirties when she was murdered.

CHAPTER 8

I Was at Her Mercy

ETWEEN WITNESSING MY mother's and my grandmother's abuse at the hands of men and being sexually abused myself by my two older female cousins, I
became clueless as to how to treat women or even relate to
them. What happened with my cousins at our house left me
totally wide open forever. In my world, while men controlled
women, women could still do no wrong.

My next encounter with a woman was by far the most
devastating and life-altering. It happened in 1975, when I was
nine years old and in the fourth grade: sexual abuse at the hands
of my fifteen-year-old babysitter, who was just as damaged as
I was.

Her name was Sharon White, and I was attracted to her.
She was a bit tall and sort of skinny, with brown hair, pretty
light brown eyes, and nice lips that I would always stare at. I
clearly remember how it all played out, starting with our first
encounter. I was home alone, playing with my toy, a Hot Wheels
racetrack. It was gloomy outside, a rainy day. You could hear
the rain pound on the roof. Thunder struck often, and lightning

followed. That always made me want to stay in the bed—still does to this day.

I had always enjoyed my babysitters, so when I knew this particular one could possibly come over, I'd act like I wasn't feeling well. I'd do this, just to miss school, but as a kid, I had headaches, so my mom never knew when I was faking it.

"Doubleo, get up," my mother said.

"I don't feel well. I have a headache again."

"Boy, are you serious?"

"Yeah, it's pounding pretty bad."

"Okay, stay in the bed. I'll call Sharon to see if she can come babysit you." My mother got ready to go to work. My siblings had already gone to school, and my father was gone as well. "She'll be here shortly. Be good now, okay?"

"Okay, Mommy, I will be," I responded. I did plan to be good, with the exception of staring at the babysitter when she arrived. That was innocent.

Not long after my mother left, I peeked out the window in anticipation of Sharon's arrival, like a happy little puppy bouncing around and standing up on its hind legs to get a snack. Babysitters gave me comfort. I was at peace when they came around, and always had a warm feeling. But on that particular day, though I didn't know it, this babysitter had more than just babysitting on her mind.

I saw Sharon approach our house. She walked up the sidewalk leading to our front door. My mother was already in the car in the driveway, ready to leave. I crouched down, as if I wasn't waiting for Sharon, but I was eagerly anticipating her arrival.

The doorbell chimed. *Dingdong.*

I answered, acting as if I had just woken up. "Hi, Sharon, come on in." I stood behind the door, and she entered.

"Thanks," she said. "I hear you have a headache."

"Yeah, it's pounding pretty bad."

"Okay, we'll fix that," was her response. She turned and waved at my mother.

My mother blew the horn and waved back just as she was leaving.

Sharon shut the door. "Are you hungry?"

"Yeah. Can I have some cereal or a snack?"

"Sure. Let's go to the kitchen."

She looked in the cabinets as I stood there waiting in anticipation, ready to eat, and gazing at her toned brown legs from behind.

"Aha, got it. You want some of these cookies?"

"Sure, why not? Chocolate chips are my favorite."

"Okay, let me get you some milk, too."

"Cool, they taste even better with milk."

"You wanna go in the living room, or the basement?"

"Living room is fine," I replied.

"Okay, let's go."

After about twenty minutes, Sharon seemed antsy, not calm at all. It just seemed weird to me.

"Doesn't seem like anything is on TV," she said. "Wanna go downstairs?" She smirked.

"You know I'm scared to go down there by myself, but since you're here, let's go."

We didn't have much in our basement. It was cold on most days, clammy, and clothes were everywhere. There was a long, light-purple couch, a washer, dryer, piles of newspapers, an old black-and-white TV with a hanger sticking out of the back wrapped with aluminum foil, and most of our toys—nothing to look forward to, really.

I found it odd that Sharon would grab me by the hand and escort me down the stairs as we made our way down, but she grabbed me in what seemed like a loving, caring way, and it did feel good. Once downstairs, we sat around, and she turned on the TV. I continued to eat my cookies and drink my milk, legs crossed on the couch, flicking my toes. I felt like a little man in her company, and it seemed as if she felt the same.

"You wanna play house?" she asked me.

"House? How so? Who am I, and who are you?"

"You're Dad, and I'm Mom, okay?"

I instantly felt an uneasy feeling come over me. I was nervous, but excited at the same time. My mind quickly went into a mode of parenting, so it seemed almost easy to play like I was a father. "Okay, I'm Dad, but where are the kids?" I asked her.

My asking this question prompted her to look into my eyes. What did I know about looking into a woman's eyes? Nothing, but it sure felt good because her eyes were light brown, and she was actually a cute girl.

"Come here, Doubleo," she said. "Scoot over close to me."

I put my glass of milk down and nervously scooted over next to her. She pulled my jaws and face to hers so close I could feel her breath warm against my skin, and I grabbed her face.

"Little boy, who taught you that?"

"Taught me what?" I replied.

"How to grab a girls face. You've done that to someone before, haven't you?"

I slowly put my head down in shame. "Yeah, my cousins used to cover my mouth a lot. They would grab my face like you did and put their mouth . . . well, you know, so that's how I learned."

"I liked it," she confessed. "Do it again."

"Can I tell you something?" I asked.

"Sure, go ahead," she replied.

"Well, I liked it then, and like it now," I told her.

"Really? You like it with me, too?"

We grabbed each other's face again. It seemed like for hours. That was all I knew how to do, at that moment.

"Lean back," she told me.

"Uh, okay." I began to get nervous, and my heart started to pump vigorously.

She leaned over, and then leaned back. Then she took my arm and wrapped it around her neck and brought my torso closer to hers. I could feel and hear her heart beating just as fast as mine.

"You know what's next, right?" she asked me

"Kind of . . . like what my parents do," I said. "But I'm scared."

My heart was racing, my palms now sweating. We were both on the couch. Then she lay all the way back. The next thing I knew, she was making me have sex with her. I remember thinking how bad this was, and how horrible I felt. I was a child, and I had no idea what I was doing except that she was making me do it.

This went on for months, right in our household, and over time, even though it was wrong, I started loving it. She was my babysitter, and that's what babysitters were supposed to do, right? They were supposed to take care of you. That was my thinking.

After we were done, we got dressed and didn't say a word, just headed back upstairs and sat around waiting for my siblings or parents to come home.

"Don't tell anyone, okay? If you do, I won't babysit you ever again."

"Okay, I won't." I never said anything to anyone. Never! I shut down, but not with her. I was deeply turned on, and yes, at age nine, kids do get horny, just so you know.

The more she came over, the better it seemed things got. After a few encounters, she stepped things up. One time she brought over some movies. This made things incredibly intense for me. I can remember looking at the cover, flipping it over, reading about the scenes, the actors, and looking at the positions on the cover. Before I knew it, we were watching adult movies.

Throughout my younger years, this sexual relationship deeply affected me and altered my way of thinking. Never would I have thought to look at her in a sexual way. After all, she was trusted to take care of me, feed me, help me bathe, and go over my homework. After that first time having sex with her, though, sex was all that I thought about.

She changed my way of thinking when it came to women and sex. At first, I embraced my loss of innocence, welcoming it as a badge of honor because I was experiencing the same thing that older men were experiencing. Each time, when we were done having sex, she always wanted to cuddle, and I did so, even though I didn't want to. I felt bad, as if I had betrayed my parents and my siblings. To me, sex with an older woman meant that I was ready for any woman. Although she was just a teenager herself, to me, sexually, she was a woman. I never had a chance to make a choice. I took the experience for what it was and took it to be the right thing.

She gave me comfort and hope, and as crazy as it sounds, I did feel safe when I was with her. After you've lived in a violent household, you look for other things to not only make you feel good, but to take your mind off the brutalities of your daily existence. I remember my father beating my mother, choking her, pulling her hair, slapping her, and yelling, which always scared the hell out of me. I remember my mother hitting my father as well, so it wasn't a one-way fight, not ever.

When I was molested, I never thought to tell my parents. Both parents worked hard, and they had their own issues, as well. The fighting, lying, late night jobs, a host of things. Drugs, alcohol . . . so many things going on that they were too blinded by their own pain to see mine. They didn't know what I was going through.

I had no idea how to cope with the struggles that I went through in my family, and this dysfunctional sexual relationship with my babysitter became a welcome distraction from it all. I remember her quite clearly: her extremely developed body, pretty eyes, and thick red lips. When it was time for her to come over and babysit me, she always wore bright red lipstick. It followed every curve and outline of her lips, filling in all of their fullness. Her hair was fairly short, flipped up around the edges, a streaked shade of golden brown. It lay on the top of her shoulders. Her skin was tan, like a mocha color, and smooth as silk. To me, she seemed much wiser than I was, and she was older, taller, and more experienced. I was still a virgin, as most nine-year-olds are, when she started babysitting me, but as I've said, that changed. I turned into a sexual deviant, and this would affect me for the rest of my life.

My understanding of what was happening to me as I was being molested by my babysitter is complicated. I wish I could say that I hated every second of it, but the truth is that I didn't. When babysitting days would come around, I couldn't wait for my parents to leave home. I remember Sharon smiling in my mother's face every time my mother left me with her. She was extremely happy, and so was I. My mother had no clue. As soon as we were alone, I knew what was up, and so did Sharon.

The molestation was the beginning of a long and extremely painful journey for me. In the years that followed, I became lost. I didn't know how to keep a relationship. Getting women always felt easy to me, but keeping them was a greater challenge. I knew at an early age exactly what to do to gain their attention—at least for girls my age—and turn them on.

My juvenile flirting concealed mannish, naughty thoughts

that I was far too young to have. Maybe there was something going on in Sharon's household, too. Who knows? At any rate, I was hers, she wasn't mine, and I was stuck. Throughout our time in that neighborhood, it would piss me off to see her with any guy her own age because I knew what he was getting. I didn't want her to have a boyfriend, nor did I like to see men her age around her. In my twisted little mind, she was no longer my babysitter, but my older girlfriend.

I know how it feels to be heartbroken. I learned at an early age, not just from family, but from an older woman who took my virginity, heart, mind, body, and soul. I was already lost, but she took it to another level. What she did to me, I carried with me for years to come. Nasty thoughts, desires to be with women—especially older ones—I carried these things with me as no child ever should. I should have gotten help, but with my household in disarray, who could I turn to?

Now that I'm older and wiser, I have more respect for my body and mind. Now I hate Sharon for doing that to me.

I spent much of my life believing that sexually, my molestation had helped me. In my mind, even at nine years old, I felt as if I was experienced. A woman wanted me and gave herself to me. I gave myself to her—but it destroyed me. From that period of life and years into my adulthood, I felt the aftermath of this experience. Sex became the leading factor upon which I based my relationships. *Money rules the world*, I thought, *and so does sex.* She took away my ability to learn how to treat a lady, my ability to know what was important in a relationship, and my chance to learn what was not. In my mind, if you had plump lips and a hairy pussy, you were mine.

From my molestation came many drawbacks later on in life. I didn't know how to do the little things like open doors for women, hold hands, or even say good morning. I hated doing those things for them because I felt like I didn't need to. I was already being satisfied, and in my mind, so were they. I didn't realize that a relationship is based on more than sex. That's how warped my mind was. I didn't care to experience a woman's emotional, spiritual, or financial needs. My mind was corrupted. I had been allowed to do the bare minimum and get away with it. I sought out women who had low self-esteem, maybe because they were poor, had been abused themselves, or they needed money. They were willing to accept less.

It took me a long time to pull out of this nose dive. I had to learn not only the components of a relationship, but the ways of a woman. I had to learn to understand her desires, wants, needs, and the way that she communicates. I had to learn to become a great listener, even when she wasn't saying anything. Body language is a lost art, and so is listening to a woman. I never saw these things done for my mother unless there was a man who wanted her. Then he would act as if he possessed those qualities, but it was all just a ruse. I watched the men say nice things, open doors, and even pull out my mother's chair in an attempt to win her over sexually, but it had no impact on me. That crap meant nothing to me. For years, because of being molested, I hated to cuddle with a woman. I hated it so much that when I did, which wasn't often, I'd feel suffocated, trapped, and I fought it for years. Cuddling actually made me angry.

Molestation—if it was bad for me, why did I go along with it in the first place? *Do what she said*, I thought, not because I was scared, but because I didn't want Sharon to stop or not come see me again. This was our secret, and she made my rough, scary days better. She took my mind off of that house, those horrific nights of my parents fighting, and just the thoughts of being dysfunctional.

I never told my parents about this, and to this day, only a few of my friends know about it. My molester is still around, though I haven't seen her in years. I've always wondered what the conversation would be like if I encountered her. I've even wondered what feelings would come back. Would I be angry? Excited? Would I want to show her what I now know about sex? Would I report her?

All of those questions have circled my mind for more than forty years. What would I do? Would I look at her nice lips again? I have no clue how many times the molestation actually happened, just that it happened time and time again, and it seemed like it went on for days, months, or even years. In the short term, she helped me by taking my mind off my dysfunctional household, but the relief was short-lived, and in the long run, the molestation only made my problems worse. Once I had been molested, not only did I have to deal with my parents arguing and fighting, I now had a really bad secret, something so bad that my babysitter could have gone to jail for it.

What should I have done? I thought that she was my peace of mind, my solace, my protector, my lover, and my all. It got to the point where I hardly cared what went on in my household, as long as she came by to babysit me. Still, to this day I ask myself, *Why me?* I had a brother her age. Why didn't she choose him? That would have been consensual at best—no harm, no foul—and surely no trouble. But I was the one, maybe the one for her at that time and age.

At some point, Sharon stopped being nice to me when she came over. There was no more playing house, no more eating cookies, just sex. She wasn't gentle anymore, either. Each time, she became more and more aggressive and less nice. As her anger grew, so did my fear of telling. I felt trapped, guilty, but as weird as it may sound, I felt obligated to have sex with her, as if she was doing me a favor. My mind processed care, and not the removal of my innocence or virginity.

CHAPTER 9

Grown-Lady Crush

THANKS TO MY cousins, I went into elementary school attracted to older women. Thankfully, my first grade teacher wasn't attractive—at least not to me—so she couldn't keep my attention sexually. However, after being kissed and sucked on at such an early age, the urge and desires were still there, so I found a way to look at and flirt with the girls in my class.

One day, a few friends and I even had the shit spanked out of us. The teacher did it because we were looking under a girl's skirt. I couldn't help it. The desire to do that was very strong. Of course, my parents were told about the incident, and I got my ass kicked when I got home, too. To think that this all went down when I was only in the first grade.

* * *

My third grade teacher, Mrs. Kay (not her real name) was a strong-willed lady, very smart, and very tough. She was nice-looking, too, with long, pretty black hair and those plump lips that I loved. I would watch her every move. She had a good body, thick thighs, and to me, perfect breasts. She didn't play at all: if we stepped out of line, we got our asses handed to us. For that reason, I also thought that she was the meanest lady on earth.

Soon enough, though, another woman caught my eye: my teacher's counterpart. She was another nice-looking lady, with curvy hips, long hair, and again those nice lips. I could feel the attraction again. I know it sounds incredible today that I was thinking these things as a school-aged child, but my way of thinking had been totally altered by my youthful introduction to sex. Everything I felt at the time seemed good and strong and even normal to me. I knew that my babysitter's actions had been wrong, but my body felt like it needed this demon, and I loved it.

The other third grade teacher had some nice qualities, too. She would always smell so good, and in my twisted mind, she was wearing that perfume just for me, those tight jeans just for me, and keeping her hair down just for me. Anyone could have told me how wrong this was, but I wouldn't have believed them. The truth is that as wrong as it was, this was my comfort zone and my way of coping with dysfunction. It was my motivation for wanting to go to school each day.

I would actually come up with plans to be alone with her. Back then, teachers could swat kids on their butts with a paddle for acting up. My teacher didn't usually have any reason to paddle me, so I had to come up with a plan for her to do so. As painful as it was, my plan worked. I would throw an eraser, make jokes, laugh, sharpen my pencil when she was trying to talk, do anything so that she'd have to spank me. Once a student did something wrong, it was the teacher's duty to take them back into the coatroom, make them bend over, and give them the swats on their ass. I knew that would hurt, but my mind was on her being in a room all alone with me. She had no clue what I was thinking.

The teachers were required to adjust the students' pants before they swatted them. To do so, they would have to get close to us, make sure our pants were on the right way, zipped up, and snug. As my teacher would come to adjust my pants, I would of course try and make it harder for her, just so that I could smell her perfume longer. She would tussle with me until she felt my pants were adjusted properly.

I didn't care about the adjustments or the swats. All I wanted to do was smell her perfume and feel her silky hair brush up against my face as she tried to adjust my pants. After the swatting ended, I distinctly remember staring at her and being upset, but at the same time enjoying the fact that I was in a room alone, one-on-one, with a nice-looking older woman. She and I would tussle so hard that her perfume stayed on my hands and clothes. I would enjoy that smell the entire day.

Truthfully, I only did well in her class because I was attracted to her. Good or bad, she'd give me attention—and the good behavior was often followed by awards and hugs. I didn't care about an award. I just wanted to be close to her. It was sad. I was happy.

CHAPTER 10

Lost, Confused, and Damaged

Don't think about who you were.
Think about who you shall become.

MY FATHER WAS a dog lover, so in addition to the cats, frogs, hamsters, and turtles that we had in our house when I was growing up, we always had dogs at home throughout my childhood. Having animals became a soothing escape and an outlet for me. They were my playmates, and they brought a sense of normalcy to my world.

Like any child, I had a natural curiosity about how animals reproduce and give birth to their young, and when I was nine years old, I finally had the chance to witness the miracle of life. I can distinctively remember my dog Sheba howling in the middle of the night. I woke up, grabbed my father's flashlight, and went into the garage, surprised to see little puppies popping out, one after another, until she didn't have the strength to push anymore.

As I stood there watching my dog suffer and struggle to give birth, I began to cry because she seemed so helpless and in pain. She appeared to be asking me for help. In a rush to save her litter, I began to help Sheba deliver the puppies, thirteen of them, all in a matter of a few hours. I was in such amazement that I hardly realized it was extremely early in the morning. I had school the next day, and I was a mess. As the puppies crawled around looking for their mother to feed them, I rushed into the house to find an old blanket to keep her and the puppies warm. No one knew where I had been or what had transpired.

Delivering puppies was a rare and special moment in my life that made me feel important. I finally felt like I meant something—even if only to my dog. I no longer felt lost, confused, or scared. I found happiness in helping. The experience of delivering the puppies was a relief of sorts for me. It was amazing that I could do that, and that Sheba had allowed me to. I wish this feeling had lasted longer, but it was only a short time before my life once again took a turn for the worse.

Life is full of little things.
Little things are full of life.

CHAPTER 11

Losing My Father

İT WAS LATE 1976, heading into 1977, fall and close to wintertime. Here's how it all went.

When kids in our neighborhood heard about a Halloween party at our house, they filled the basement, yelling and screaming, giving high fives, just ecstatic. Cars lined the driveway, and parents kissed their kids and headed out.

My best buddies ran up the driveway, shouting my name. "Doubleo, are you ready to have fun?" they asked, smiling, and laughing.

"Heck, yeah," I replied. "Let's go inside, man."

We waved to their parents and headed down into our basement.

"Man, that costume is cool," I told my buddy. "Turn around. Let me check it out."

My friend spun around, then stopped, spread his arms, and said, "It's cool, right?"

"Yeah, man, I like it."

My mother had candy and decorations, and all sorts of festivities went on at once. Hot food, apple cider—you name it, we had it all. Bobbing for apples was my favorite game. Each kid took a turn trying to get the apples out of a metal tub filled with ice-cold water.

"Toni," I shouted, "your turn."

"Okay, cool," my sister replied. She dunked her head into the tub of water and came up with a fat, juicy apple protruding from her mouth/

"Yay," we all shouted, jumping, screaming, and laughing.

"Who's next?" my mother asked.

"Not me," my little friend Charles said. "I ain't messin' up my Afro, man."

"Yeah, don't put your greasy head in that water. I don't want your nasty hair in my mouth."

We laughed and kept going with the night's festivities.

My mother had kids over because she loved to entertain—something that my father and sisters enjoyed as well. Not only did she like to have company, but my mother also cooked and managed the night's events, making sure that everyone had a great time. We always had birthday parties, cookouts, celebrations, and anything else that my mother could do to keep us involved in things and to keep the kids all together inside the house. It worked well and kept my mind off the arguments and fights. We had animals, a basketball court in the backyard, a seemingly endless food supply, great music, and plenty of things to do.

It was a good thing my father worked the night shift at Ford, because most times when he came home, that was it: lights out, kids gone, fun was over. The night shift did us well. We loved my father, but it was difficult for him to tolerate our parties after working twelve to fifteen hours in the foundry.

The fear of seeing my father pissed off terrified me. If we were playing in the backyard and I saw my father's car pull into the driveway, I immediately felt like I had to pee. I'm not sure if I was afraid of him, or afraid of him having another violent fight with my mother. Whatever the feeling was, it was sickening every time. From a block or so away, I could hear my father driving down the street, slowly cruising. He'd always blast his music, either the Temptations, the Four Tops, Smokey Robinson, or the O'Jays. Those were his favorites.

On this day of the Halloween party, I distinctly remember hearing the song "Still Waters Run Deep" by the Four Tops. I loved hearing music blast from the speakers in his car, but it always came with an eerie feeling. I wondered how he would be when he pulled up. Would he be drunk, would he become violent, or would he be crying from the pain of our dysfunctional family? I'd often catch my father shedding tears, alone, all by himself, or sitting with our dogs. It was really sad. As strong and as powerful as my father was, he still had a soft side.

Sometimes, when he'd pull up, I'd go outside before he could get out of his car and wait for him in the backyard. I'd hide behind a tree and listen to him either weep or talk to the dogs. I didn't know which to expect. When he talked to the dogs, I knew he was drunk. Talking to the dogs soothed his pain.

The night of the Halloween party, I saw that ugly-ass blue Catalina pull up into the driveway. My father opened the driver's door, one leg hanging out. He paused for a moment, and when he did, I automatically felt nervous, scared, and sick. It seemed like he was pausing to gather his thoughts, thinking of how he could ruin a party, whip us, or start an argument with my mother.

"Doubleo," he yelled, "come here."

I ran as fast as I could to the open door.

"What's going on in the house? Where's your mother?"

I turned to look back toward the house. "She's in there, Daddy. Are you okay?"

"Nah, man, I'm not," he said, his head held low. "I'm not."

"We're having a Halloween party. Is that okay, Daddy?"

I smelled alcohol on his breath. He'd worn his favorite Ford Motor Company blue coveralls, and he smelled like hot steel from the foundry. I knew he was tired. I paid more attention to the scowl on his face as he got out of the car and looked at me.

"Hell, nah, that ain't okay. I worked all damn day. Nah, it ain't okay. I'm tired. Shit."

Fear started to grow inside me as I wasn't sure what was next. I had come to know that liquor smell so well that I could recognize Seagrams Gin reeking from his breath a mile away—and I would begin pissing my pants from the thought of what could go wrong. What was he about to do? Would we get our asses spanked?

I feared my father, but I also loved him dearly. I didn't want to see him angry, so pissing my pants wasn't a problem for me. It was like I was admitting to defeat. Letting him down had become the norm. I'd much rather get people out of our backyard, out of the house, and clean the house in pissy pants, than face his wrath or let him down.

"All right, man, I'm going in the backyard with the damn dog."

I walked with my father to the backyard. He stumbled a little, sat down, and rubbed our dogs, Duke and Sheba, as he talked to them. His strokes on the dogs' fur appeared to feel soothing to them. I sat there with him for a few minutes, anxiously waiting for him to fall asleep on the old rusty barbecue pit that rested against the garage so I could go back inside and have fun. Looking back, it doesn't make much sense, but I was a child at the time, and children's minds can work in mysterious ways. The dogs soothed my father's pain, just as he soothed theirs.

My father was a solid man—tall, dark, and built. Women loved him, especially when he wore his blue Ford Motor Company coveralls. Most of the time when he came home, as

I mentioned, he smelled like he'd been dipped in a barrel of liquor. He drank his ass off—we knew this—and it might have been every single day. Luckily for us, when he was on the night shift, we didn't always have to see him. On most nights, the night shift worked in our favor.

* * *

In the fall of 1977, I would soon turn twelve, and we were having one of the kids' parties that my mother loved so much to host. Most of the time, the kids all went home after the parties, with the occasional exception of one or two who either didn't want to go home or didn't have any place to go afterward. All the parents knew our house was a good enough place to leave their kids. That's what they thought, anyway—that the kids were in my mother's good hands. They ate well, and they had fun. They had no clue who I really was.

Don't get me wrong. My mother did her part as far as showing us attention, managing all the kids, keeping order, feeding everyone, handling the events, and even using discipline when needed. What she didn't know was that prior to these parties, I had been watching porn and my preteen hormones were out of control. I was now in the sixth grade, still much too young to even know about sex, hormones, or any other related adult matters. Still, the thing is that I was not a normal kid. I knew far too much about sex for my own good, and it was showing through my secret behaviors.

There was more conflict brewing under the surface. While the other kids' parents thought of our house as a good place to leave their kids for the night, tensions were building up behind the scenes. My father was barely around, not only because he had been working his ass off, but because my parents were also pursuing a divorce. It's something that would later haunt me for the rest of my life. As the talk of divorce found its way around our family, we kids weren't ready for it. My siblings and I weren't privy to what exactly was going on. All we knew was that things were different at home: tensions were high, food was scarce, and not many kids were coming over. Not just the food was scarce. Money was low, and our utilities were being shut off. Not having a father in the home meant that a lot would be missing. His steady hand and strict discipline were missed, and our income was drastically reduced by more than half.

My mother didn't have the time to look after us the way she had before. Don't get me wrong. Women are just as capable as men of running a household, but this was back in the '70s. Things were different back then. Although my mother tried her best to keep our house under control, even her best wasn't good enough to manage everything. She had three kids, dogs, reptiles, hamsters, and one mannish little boy to contend with. (That part, she had no clue about.) As the divorce transpired, we felt the ill effects of a dysfunctional household. The fear of my father had dissipated. The sight of him driving down the street in the big-ass blue car was no longer. His coveralls were gone, his laughter was missing, his presence had vanished, and we were in shambles.

My friends laughed at me when my parents divorced, and that was extremely painful. When parents divorce, no one really knows the first order of effect that it has.

At school when we had to write down our parents' status, the question inevitably arose: Are your parents married or divorced? Every time I had to answer that question, I would cry. The teachers, counselors, and Little League coaches would look at me and try to comfort me, but it didn't do any good. What I am saying is this: when parents get divorced, the kids have to answer questions on school registrations, sports registrations, job applications (back then for summer jobs), getting an ID to be able to swim at the local pool, and many other things.

I hated seeing that question over and over again, and this went on forever, it seemed. I hated answering the question about my parents' divorce because it seemed as if when the supervisors read my applications and other parental forms, they'd look at me as if I was a hopeless, dysfunctional little boy who came from a broken family—and I was.

It was almost as if the world was saying to me, "If your parents are divorced, you are dirty, unfit, and lost." That was how I felt every time I had to answer that question, and I felt like I had to answer it all the time.

One memory stands out in my mind. I don't remember where I was or what the circumstances were—I just remember a lady yelling out loud, "If your parents are divorced, stand in the next line."

I recall thinking to myself, *What a bitch! How dare she separate us.*

Every time something of that nature happened, I'd try to stay in the lines for kids of married parents, hoping and praying that I wouldn't be separated from the kids who had married parents. Again, I felt disgusting, and pushed to the side. It was only later that I discovered the real reason we had to stand in another line: without a father in the home, our household income had been drastically reduced, and we needed financial assistance. That's what the whole business was about. So, needless to say, we went through a lot of changes when my parents divorced. The whole household dynamic changed.

Another major change that I went through when my father left was that with him went my access to pornography. Before my parents divorced and my father left the house, I had been watching porn—since the tender young age of nine. When my father was still around, we had an extra TV, and that was the one that I would use to sneak and watch the porn videos on. It began with various white women and planted a desire in me for older women, period.

My babysitter was the one who first introduced me to porn, and the hard-core, rough, and raw scenes of group sex and bestiality etched themselves into my memory. The first scene I can recall was a threesome involving two white women and a black man. I had no idea of what to do with what I was seeing or how to handle the situation. I had no clue why it was being shown to me at all. Still, I enjoyed the hell out of it. I became addicted to porn right at that moment. Nine years old, inexperienced, excited, and scared, with thoughts racing, my young mind and body struggled to make sense of what I was seeing and feeling.

Once my father left, the porn stopped. He left us with only one television, which the whole family shared. I had no place left to go and sneak the porn. I couldn't be alone, and my family members were no longer distracted. Still, as I mentioned before, it was too late. I was an addict, and I needed to find another way to get my fix. If it wasn't porn, I had to find another way to fill my appetite for sexual things.

CHAPTER 12
Glory Hole

THROUGHOUT MY CHILDHOOD, I sought comfort and escape from the family turmoil and violence that surrounded me. Having been inappropriately exposed to sex at a young age—through the encounters I've already described, and also through the porn that I found at home and became addicted to watching—I was consumed by mannish sexual desires at a very young age. Thoughts of sex gave me comfort and escape. Helping my dog deliver her puppies gave me a short break from the inappropriate thoughts of sex that normally consumed me, but unfortunately, dogs can't have puppies every day, and I was still seeking an outlet for the demons that I felt haunted my soul.

I hadn't watched porn in a long time—which is a strange thing to say about a young boy, but it's the truth regarding what my life was like—and for a while it almost felt like I had escaped my obsession with sex. All of that changed, though, because of the parties that we started to have at the house.

In 1975 or 1976, in the summertime in East Cleveland, I found my opening once my mother started having adult parties every Friday. At first, these parties felt like nothing more than a pain in the ass. The adults would come over with their liquor, weed, cocaine, and whatever else they decided to indulge in, and my house became a noisy, drug-filled, alcohol-smelling place. This drove me crazy—until a family member came up with a very bright and mannish idea. I was growing older—in the sixth grade by this point—and my hormones were really out of control. What happened next seemed like the best idea ever.

What we decided to do was drill a hole in my parents' bedroom because the wall was adjacent to the bathroom. First, we went into the bathroom to see where eye level was. Eye level to us meant that our eyesight was at the same level as the toilet where the women would sit when it was time for them to use the restroom.

This is how the plan went. Once we heard someone coming up the stairs, we would then determine if it was a man or a woman. If it was a woman, we'd signal each other and then scurry back into the corner of the master bedroom, where we could take turns looking through the hole that we had drilled in the wall. The hole was small enough that no one even knew that we were there.

What an amazing idea, I thought to myself.

I had no porn, and I had nothing to use to satisfy my lust, cravings, and desire to see women. Through that hole in the bathroom wall, though, I gained access to the real thing. Something that I had only previously seen in movies was now in front of me in real life.

This game became so addictive that we would fight over how long each person could look through the wonderful hole, which I now know was called a "glory hole." I distinctly remember seeing the first grown lady that entered the bathroom in my mother's house. She was a very nice-looking lady who had a wonderful laugh, short hair, big beautiful lips, smooth pecan-colored skin, and she was married. Those weren't her only qualities. I'll call her Trina. She would often come to our house for most anything, and every time she came over, she'd always wear these nice, tight, and short skirts that would show every inch of her thick, wide ass.

During those visits, I could only imagine what she really looked like undressed. Yes, I was attracted to older women, even at an early age. This is what happens when you watch porn at the ripe age of nine years old.

Trina was very pretty, confident, had a nice job, and always brought me gifts. Friday night, the party would be jumping, with people smoking and drinking a lot, so I knew that we would get an eyeful of butt and vagina all night long.

Our first victim was Trina, then Daisy, and then I remember Cherry. Trina had a nice smooth butt, with an unshaved vulva area later in life, I loved a hairy vulva because of Trina. Our next victim was Daisy. She was a short lady, with short hair, nice lips, and curvy hips. She had skin the color of cocoa brown and loved to smoke. There was also Cherry, who would come into the bathroom and get totally naked. She had very nice breast with dark brown circles and thick nipples.

Damn, I can't wait to be grown, I remember thinking.

For hours on end we watched these women undress, swing their butt around, and wipe their vagina. I remember watching so long that my eyes would swell. I knew right then that I had an addictive personality. That part of me comes from my mother.

So that was the way it happened. I came to expect the thrill of watching the women through the glory hole. I depended on it to satisfy what had truly become an addiction.

CHAPTER 13

The Three of Us

IN THE FALL of 1977 on Friday nights, our house was famous for house parties, the adult kind. But inevitably there came one Friday night where nothing much was going on. There was a grown-up party, but it just wasn't as fun as the previous parties. My mind was still searching for that sexual fix that I had come to rely on.

There were kids hanging around, but only allowed in the basement. We ate, played, and had a good time—but it was about to get better. While most of the kids left to go home, or their parents came to get them, one young lady stayed for the night. I'm not sure why. Throughout the party, she and I had played with each other a lot, wrestling, joking, and having a great time. She was pretty big in stature: short and thick, with a little curly Afro. Come to think of it, she was a little bit manly. Her name was Sheila. Sheila was cool. She played mostly with the boys. She was a bit tough—very strong—and she cursed like a grown man.

When she and I wrestled, I noticed that she could handle me, and for some reason, she liked to hug me in the front. I thought we were just wrestling, but I suppose in her mind it was more than that. Honestly, I was a bit scared. I didn't know what to do or think, and I wasn't sure how to act with a girl trying to wrestle me like that. Not being sure, I just went ahead and wrestled her like any other boy. The first time she got me down, she lay on top of me, not as if she was trying to win, but as if she liked me. After a few attempts to get up, I quit trying, and Sheila put her mouth on mine.

I was surprised to find that this excited me. I'm not sure why it did so much, because for the past few months all I had seen was grown women with big butts and hairy lower areas. That was what I liked, not burly young girls with brown Afros. Still, as we kept playing, a strong desire came over me. I can remember it as if it happened yesterday.

Sheila touched my mouth again, and this time I put my hands by the center of her pants, then I sniffed my fingers, and I liked it. I liked it so much that I told my friend about it.

"Man," he said, "she's been wrestling me, too. Maybe she wants both of us."

I thought to myself, *Can two guys be with a girl at the same time?* My mind quickly went back to the movies that I had seen. *Yes! That's called a threesome.*

Bedtime was quickly approaching. My hormones were racing, I was excited, and now I was beginning to like Sheila.

Well, off we all went to bed. We were in my mother's bed, me on one side, my friend on the other side, and Sheila in the middle. I remember feeling Sheila roll around, so much that I had to move over. Once I moved over, I lifted my head up and saw my buddy on top of her. They were having sex. As they lay there, I heard Sheila speak softly—pure ecstasy. This, of course, turned me on, so much so that I sat up and started to watch them. I became more and more excited as I watched them. They were both virgins before that night, but not anymore.

We were totally unsupervised. My sister was in her room, my mother had left for the night, and my father no longer lived there.

Sheila asked me to join in. "When Jerry gets off," she said, "I want you on top of me."

I obliged without hesitation. We were out of control from that point on.

We had all just had our first threesome, and we were only in the sixth grade. After that night, the threesomes continued, and it became a regular thing. My friend and I would have sex with Sheila weekly, and it became something that we all enjoyed. After a certain point, it was hard to stop. We didn't think twice about stopping at all. And that's how it all happened: my demons were even more deeply rooted by the time I was only in the sixth grade.

We would all suffer the effects of this early sexual activity for years to come. The saddest part about it was that after my friend and I stopped having sex with Sheila, it got around the neighborhood that she was sexually active. There were a few grown men much older than myself and my buddy who started having sex with her as well. To this day, I truly believe that what we did to and with her eventually caught up to her in a way that drove her away from men altogether. She was done with men, at least sexually. Sadly, I feel that I had a lot to do with this, and I feel horrible about it. During my quest over the years to try to right my wrongs, what happened to Sheila would always come to mind, just randomly, so I knew that I had to talk about it. I had to find Sheila.

Eventually, I did. It was 2007. I looked her up on the Internet and called her from home. The conversation was extremely odd. How could it not have been? I had no clue how to start it. I didn't know if she had gone through therapy, if she would talk to me, or how she would feel.

"Sheila?" I began hesitantly. "This is Leon Walker. I don't know if you remember me or not."

"I remember you," she said in a guarded voice.

It was clear I'd piqued her interest, but she was going to let me do all the talking, at least to start.

After some small talk, I drummed up the courage to broach our sordid past. "I know it's been a long time, but I've been thinking a lot about the old neighborhood, about some of the things that happened, you know, growing up. What happened between us, it, well . . ."

"You don't owe me an apology," she said. "That was a long time ago."

"Maybe so," I said, "but that kind of thing stays with you for the rest of your life. It's taken me years, but I'm just now coming to grips with everything I did back then. I guess I wish I could have been a better friend to you."

That was all it took to open the floodgates, and next thing I knew, Sheila was reliving her childhood.

"You weren't the only one with issues," she said. "My daddy was never around. I think I was looking for a connection—any kind of connection—with a boy. It was wrong. I know that now. But at the time, I just wanted to be close to someone."

"I get that," I said. "From my end, I wish our home could've been, you know, a safe haven for you."

"It was," she said. "Most of the time."

"I didn't make it any safer," I said, my voice cracking with guilt. "I made it worse by giving you back exactly what you were running from."

"You were just a kid."

"Eleven years old and dysfunctional as hell. Add to that, damaged and confused. I didn't know how to support you or respond to your fears. I guess I had my own to contend with. I couldn't be the friend you needed."

"We used each other," she said, as if attempting to claim some responsibility. "I was a comfort to you, and you were a comfort to me."

That made me feel a little better. We talked for several more minutes, updating each other on our lives. And after we hung up, I heaved a long sigh. I was glad I'd risked calling her.

Talking to Sheila helped, but nothing can change the fact that I still feel bad about what happened to this day. As for Sheila, she's now a lesbian, and she has never had any kids.

CHAPTER 14

I'm Going to Kill
Your Father

My fathers spirit could have left his body right here

Control who you are,
and who you are then becomes controlled by you.

S EX SHOULDN'T BE natural to a child, but it was to me because it was all that I knew. The same could be said for violence. I grew up around it, and it was part of the only world that I knew.

It was late fall of 1978, close to Thanksgiving. I remember being home alone and going into my mother's room. I stood in front of the mirror, acting out a scene in my mind, like cops and robbers. There was an old hat that my father had left in my mother's closet. It was black leather, and leaning to the side. That was the way he wore his hats. I slid it on my head. It barely stayed on. Then I put on his black leather jacket, that he had also left. As I was wearing my underwear, and nothing else, I didn't feel quite complete.

In my mind, I was the robber, and there was a cop in front of me, but I needed a weapon. Looking in my mother's drawer, sifting past her clothes, bras, stockings, and jewelry, I found a gun. It was a nice gun, too. I looked at the bullets and held them in my hands. They seemed huge to me. The gun was heavy, cold, and very intimidating. It was dark blue in color, and smelled like steel. I took it out and waved it around like I was really going to do something with it, playing cops and robbers alone.

"Put your hands up, man," the cop said.

"Nah, you put your hands up," I barked back.

The make-believe cop and I went back and forth for a few minutes. Then I acted like I was slowly running away from the make-believe scene, shooting back as I made my getaway. I aimed the gun at the mirror, but it was empty. I stopped, snapped out the chamber of the gun, spun it quickly around, loaded my invisible bullets in, snapped it back in, and kept shooting at the mirror, as if I was a cool western gunslinger.

I was having a blast—until my mother came in and caught

me with it. The door swung open, *shoosh*. My eyes popped out of my head, my hand covered my mouth, and I froze stiff.

"Boy, if you don't put that damn gun down . . ." My mother's mouth closed tightly as she walked up on me, eyes piercing mine. "What are you doing, Doubleo?"

I could clearly hear her every word.

"I'm going to beat your ass!"

"Okay, Mommy, I'm sorry."

"And take off those damn clothes!" she shouted. "As a matter of fact, throw them away. They're old and dirty."

I got my ass beat that day—probably not even for playing with the gun, but for the fact that now someone other than my mother knew that there was a gun in the house. She gave me an eerie look, as if she was thinking, *That gun is for your father*, but she never said as much.

* * *

Pow, pow, pow, pow, pow, pow. I heard gunshots. My sister and I were at Daisy's house, spending the night with her kids.

"Toni, did you hear that," I asked.

"Nah, what happened?"

I perked up on the bed and looked out the window in the direction of the gunshots, but I couldn't see down the street. "Somebody is shooting, down that way." I pointed toward the corner of Alder and Coit, in East Cleveland.

"Down that way?" my sister said. "Aw, man, that's close to the bar where Mommy works. I hope she's okay. Please don't let that be Mommy at the bar."

"Nooooo!" I responded, as I buried my face in the pillow. The day before the shooting, as usual, my father went off to work at Ford Motor Company, and later that night, my mother went to work at the corner bar. My father had always hated my mother working at the bar. His friends knew, and so did our friends. It was embarrassing, to say the least, and we were teased about it often. But we had no reason to think the gunshots were related to our family. I was just nervous.

With both parents off at work the day of the shooting, we were playing over at Daisy's house. It was getting later into the night, and we were still up. Back in the '70s, at least in our neighborhood, hearing gunshots was nothing extraordinary. Still, that particular night, I just knew something was wrong. With the altercation that had happened at our house the day before, I had a gut feeling that one of my parents had been killed.

Not long after hearing the gunshots, I saw three or four police cars speeding down the street.

"Toni," I said, "the police are zooming toward the bar where Mommy works. Check it out."

My sister peeped out the window. "Yeah, you're right. There's lots of cars down there, too."

We looked at each other in fear, each thinking the same thing. We both started crying, but we didn't really know why. We just had this weird feeling. I remember the red, white, and blue lights flashing everywhere. My heart was pumping fiercely as I watched them fly past Daisy's house. We still had no clue what had happened, but as I looked out the window, I could see the police crowding in the bar area.

Everyone in our neighborhood knew my parents, so it was easy for the police to find my sister, brother, and me if indeed my parents were involved. My sister and I went downstairs to see what was going on. I could see the uniformed officers through the window as I peeked out.

"Go upstairs," Daisy ordered us.

We did, but how could we stay there? I knew something had gone wrong, and I had to know what was happening. My sister and I came back downstairs every few minutes.

Bam, bam, bam came the hard knocks on Daisy's door. "Open the door. It's the police."

My sister and I looked at each other in fear. We were both shaking, and I was about to pee my pants again. That horrible feeling of fear and nervousness started to come over me. I grabbed my sister, and she grabbed me. We were in the kitchen by the back door. I could see three or four police officers dressed in uniform, burly men, and sweating. We darted back to the stairs but peeped around the corner to sneak a view.

"Come on in," Daisy said. "How can I help you?"

"We're looking for Toni and Doubleo. Are they here?"

"Yes, they're right behind me," Daisy told them. "Doubleo, Toni, come here. The police want to talk to you."

We slowly came back down the stairs.

"What happened?" I asked them. "Is everything okay?"

"No, no, it isn't. Your mother shot at your father and tried to kill him."

My sister and I burst into tears. We were shaking and holding each other.

I could barely get the words out through my tears and crying. "Wha, wha, what happened to our father? Is he okay?"

"We don't know. We can't find him. All we see are six bullet shells on the ground in and around the bar area."

I could see terror in the officer's eyes. I knew then that someone was dead. I didn't have to hear any more. I started to cry, scream, and holler. I pissed my pajamas again.

One of the officers stepped closer. He grabbed my sister and me. "Sorry to tell you this, but your mother has been arrested,"

"Noooo," my sister and I said at the same time through our tears and runny noses. "We want our mother back."

"We can't do that right now," the officer said. "She's being held for attempted murder."

I fell to my knees. My crying intensified, and through my

tears and the heartbeat pounding out of my chest, I found a way to ask again about my father. "Is he okay? Is he hurt?"

"We don't know. We can't find him. The ambulance is still searching . . . along with the police. We're looking for blood, too."

"All of those shots fired—he has to be dead!" I cried the hardest that I've ever cried. "Noooo, my father can't be dead." I looked to my left. My sister was curled up on the floor, howling in pain.

The police left Daisy's house and headed back to the scene. Hours later, there was another loud knock on the door. Daisy, my sister, and I headed back downstairs to see who it was.

"Hi, kids," the policeman said. "Just wanted you all to know that we found your father."

I looked up at him, mouth closed tight, hands clasped, leaning on Daisy for support.

She hugged me slightly. "Well, where is he?" she asked.

"He's okay. He ran out of the bar and down the street. We found his white shirt in the alley, and it does have blood on it, lots of blood."

"Is he dead?" I asked the policeman.

"Nah, but when he was trying to get away, he ran into the brick wall and got hurt trying to jump the fence in the small alley behind the bar. He's being treated now. Looks like you all will be staying over here for a while. Your mother is in jail, and your father is being treated."

Upon questioning my father, the officers had uncovered that he had left his job early, gone to the bar where my mother worked, and beat her. There wasn't a man in there who could have stopped my father from beating my mother that night, so all she could do was protect herself with that .38 revolver she kept in her purse, the same one that I had found and played with that one time in her bedroom.

The legal issues were resolved relatively quickly. My mother was jailed and released sometime later, based on self-defense, and my father was charged for assault. My mother came to Daisy's house to get us when she was released, and we went back home. Still living in fear, all we could do was hug each other that weekend and hope things would get better.

As I hugged my mother, I looked into her eyes, and I could see the pain and her swollen jaw.

She looked down at me and said, "I'm okay, Doubleo. Everything will be okay."

Looking back on it, as I do every time I visit Cleveland, the harsh reminders remain. I make it a point to visit the bar where my mother worked in East Cleveland, on the corner of Alder Avenue and Coit. I also walk the scene. I go up to the door that my father ran out of and the alley where he made his escape from the gunfire where my mother shot at him six times. The building is now demolished, but the lot is still there. When I go back to the scene, it seems as if it's frozen in time. When I get out of my truck to look at it, the memories come right back to me, a constant reminder of just one thing I went through while growing up. It's etched into my brain, and the thoughts of that night will never go away.

CHAPTER 15

His Hands on My Balls

Boy, get yo punk ass upstairs.
Lil' punk-ass nigga, I'm going to teach you a lesson.

I<small>T WAS</small> 1979. Like any other kid, I could be a smartass at times. After my father left, Marco Gates, a male family member, started coming around to visit often. He was six feet three, about 190 pounds, and had hair braided to the back and gaps in his teeth. Every tooth had a gap, and he looked like a badly carved pumpkin.

I had no clue as to why, but his visits became more and more regular. On these visits, he had something in mind—it was a gradual attack, subtle at first. Then he picked up the intensity.

I was home. It was cold outside, and I was looking out the window, as usual, when I saw a Cadillac pull up. *Cool*, I thought. *It's Marco.* Time for some food and junk.

He had other plans, though. At first things seemed to be pretty cool, good. Each time Marco came over, he'd talked to me, and we'd read comic books, though not my favorite thing to do, eat junk around the house, and just be family. He even helped out around the house. My brother and sister were always there, so to me, nothing seemed out of the ordinary at all.

But things started to change when I began to find myself alone with him. Never in my life did I imagine that a family member would do such a thing to me, but I quickly found out that the word "family" didn't mean anything to him.

Everyone was gone. My mother was at work, and my siblings were outside playing.

He whispered to me, "Pssst, Doubleo, go upstairs."

I didn't know why he was whispering. Maybe he thought that my siblings were in the basement.

"Go upstairs for what," I asked.

He looked at me, his face angrily wrinkled. "Just do what the fuck I'm telling you, nigga."

A horrible feeling came over me, and I started to shake. I got to the top of the stairs and turned around to find him close, right in my face.

He grabbed me by the collar, slapped me, and commanded, "Take your ass into the bathroom and get some Vaseline, bitch."

I started crying because I knew that this wasn't normal, and something bad was about to happen. We were alone, and he could overpower me at any time.

It was a gradual attack, subtle at first. Then he picked up the intensity. I proceeded to go into the bathroom to get the Vaseline and walked out to find him lying on the floor with his pants down to his knees. He was looking back at me while lying on his stomach.

"Rub the Vaseline on my butt," he said. "Rub the Vaseline on my butthole area."

I instantly felt sick. *This is wrong*, I thought. I refused to do it. "Nope," I snapped back. "Hell, no, you nasty Marco."

"Boy, do what the fuck I'm telling you," he said as he lay on the floor.

I wanted to stomp his ass right there, but I was too scared.

He stood up, pants down to his knees, but I wouldn't look

down at his penis, not at all. He was much older, taller, and stronger than me. All I could do was *not* take my pants down, and I didn't.

Crack. He slapped me. And every time I refused, he slapped me on the head and then punched me in the stomach. I cried hard as hell, holding my stomach and head, and trying to get away.

"Come here, boy," he whispered. "Do what the fuck I tell you, boy."

"No!" I yelled. Each time I cried and yelled, he would cover my mouth and I would bite the hell out of him. I gripped the Vaseline in my hand. We scuffled back and forth.

"Gimme the Vaseline, punk-ass nigga. Give it here."

"No, no, no, get off of me," I yelled through his hands that covered my mouth. As I stood there taking the punishment, all I could do was think about how vulnerable I was because my father wasn't home any longer, and how, if he had been, this would not have been happening. I was pissed at my mother for divorcing my father and leaving me and my siblings without any protection, even though it wasn't entirely her fault.

Marco stopped for a moment. I wiped the blood from my mouth, and he tried again. My neck hurt like hell for weeks and months after that. Headaches ensued often, and my anger built. He left the house, and I never told anyone.

I couldn't wait to get older so I could beat his ass, or even better, get my mother's gun and shoot him. Shooting him crossed my mind often.

But as it turned out, I wouldn't need to shoot him. More about that later.

This situation was like something you'd see in a movie. No one would believe it if you told them. It always happened when the two of us were alone. Although there was never any penetration of any kind, I was still traumatized by the event, which would haunt me for the rest of my life. Each time I refused to lie on top of him, he would slap the shit out of me. I would cry and do my best to get away.

Even then, with as much pain as I was in from him slapping me, I held my ground and felt my anger going deeper and deeper. I despised him. He always managed to come over at just the right time, always catching me home alone. His attraction to me over time started to morph into pure anger and aggression. Each time, he would become more and more aggressive, and I would fight harder and harder to get away. After he realized he couldn't put Vaseline on me and he couldn't get me to lie on top of him, he would then grab my private area and testicles through my pants with what seemed like all his might. He damn near detached that part from my body.

I hated the sight of him. I never told my parents or siblings about this monster that groped me, pulled my penis through my pants, slapped me around, and tried to make me have sex with him. He did, however, damage me for life.

Each time I got a physical for sports or for going back to school, I had to get checked by the doctor, and each time the doctor did the hernia check, he would notice that my testicles had a loose vein floating around. I lied to every doctor who examined me and never said a word about how it really happened. At that point, I had to deal with the fact that not only did Marco do damage to me mentally, but he had now also damaged me physically. I live with this to this day: some pain and some discomfort, but I manage to move forward with each day. It's a horrible reminder every time I either use the restroom or do anything that is associated with my genitals.

This all happened back in 1979, the year that a whole host of tragic and stressful things happened to me and my family: divorce, violence, torture, poverty, and even death. It's all still with me today, although I've learned to manage my misfortunes.

The memories still come back to haunt me quite often. A mind is a very precious thing, especially at such a young age. These types of experiences leave an indelible mark. I wanted to shoot him!

After being groped, I never thought that I could reproduce. It was not only a fear of mine, but I was never sure about it, and it felt like a dark secret until I had children.

CHAPTER 16

Off with His Head— Literally

I T WAS 1979, on a hot summer night back at a relative's house. It was about ten p.m., and my mother, grandmother, brother, sister, cousins, friends, and a few other family members were in the house. I was in the kitchen playing with my cousin.

The day was already coming to an end. Dinner had been served. Everyone was done eating, and we were preparing to go home—back to where we knew violence and discomfort. We had sat around and talked all day, laughing some, and witnessing my grandmother getting abused. The adults smoked, drank liquor, and laughed. For some reason, this day seemed quite odd, and I had no clue as to why. I can remember feeling happy being with family, even though people were being verbally abused. At this point, I had become used to it, and so had my sister. We blew it off as if it were the normal thing at a relative's house. All the wicked banter, a few yells and screams . . . no big deal, just another day. Nobody saw what was coming next.

The adults had been gathered in the living room, talking

about something, when they called us kids in. At this point, I had no clue where my siblings were—probably upstairs, where we spent most of our time.

Out of nowhere came my mother's harsh words: "He's dead! He's dead! Marco Gates was shot!"

As I looked up into my mother's eyes, I could see horror, pain, and sorrow. I felt extremely bad for her. This was her only friend, it seemed, and they were thick as thieves. At that instant, I felt a few things go through me: mixed feelings of happiness, sadness . . . and relief. Her friend, now dead, was the monster who had fondled me, and he was the source of so much other pain in my life. This was the one who had once thrown me around, the one who verbally abused family members, and the one who nearly snatched my penis and testicles off whenever he had the chance. Yes, the monster was Marco Gates, and he was gone, and I didn't have to shoot him like I wanted to. Someone else did.

His head had been blown off with a shotgun—a shotgun that was placed in his mouth and the trigger pulled. It happened in his apartment in Cleveland. His brains were splattered all over the wall, the table, the TV, and the floor. I'm sure blood and brains were all over the shooter as well. The shooter was supposedly known to have been his friend, partner, roommate, and lover. I'm not surprised about the lover part. As of the time of this writing, no one has ever been brought to justice.

A closed casket was called for at first, but the people at the funeral home and the morgue were able to rebuild the face and head back to what seemed to be Marco Gates in the casket.

That night and his death set off a series of events that wrecked my family, and me, forever. The year, 1979, is a year that I will never forget. We lost a close friend, and my mother's mental state started to decline, but my balls and penis were never snatched and twisted ever again. Mixed emotions, but relieved for sure !

We had gone through a lot, but we were loving

I miss these happy people

Aside from me being a bed wetter and sleepwalker, our family did have quite a few talents. My sister and I both ran track, and it turned out that we were actually pretty good at it. We competed around the Cleveland circuit and had fun doing so. Both my sister and I were built pretty thick: thick thighs and strong muscle structure, thick butts, arms, and back. We

were built from the Walker family DNA. My brother was an
artist, a talent that he was born with but used sparingly. Had he
capitalized on it, I believe to this day that he could have been a
millionaire. Instead, he chose another route.

My brother's talents are shared by my oldest son, who has
done tremendously well with art. Isn't it strange how a talent
can skip a generation and end up in the head of a child who
doesn't even belong to the person that the talent came from?
My brother had been paid as a teenager to draw, paint, and
create art pieces for grown people.

The bar that my mother worked at was the Elite, on the
corner of Alder Avenue. They needed a sign out front and asked
my brother to do it for them. He took the job, and it turned out
great. He was about seventeen or eighteen years old.

Being a kid and having your mother work as a barmaid in
the local neighborhood was embarrassing. One thing for sure,
I hated the fact that my mother was a barmaid. Eventually, she
even asked the owner to get me a job there, and he obliged,
giving me my first job at nine years old. I was required to go
there every Saturday morning to sweep the floor, wipe the
tables, clean the glasses, and wipe off the bar. It was my first job
ever, and I loved it. That was when I realized that I had a great
work ethic, and my confidence started to soar.

Of course, my confidence was always short-lived. As soon
as I gained it, I would lose it again because of my tumultuous
family life. To this day, I hate loss. I had to learn about loss—
not loss as in losing a game, but loss as in losing family, friends,
unity, and sight of what's going on. Even though I say this later
in life, I'm speaking from experience. I would eventually lose
my own family due to my infidelity. I see now that lacking the
ability to love myself, I could not love anyone, ever.

*   *   *

The greatest education

**He was tough, fair, loving, honest, strong,
and he gave us vision**

One thing has stayed with me: moving up from the fifth grade into the sixth. During the summer, and right before the beginning of the school year, no one knew who their new teacher would be. You were notified during the summer in preparation for the next school year—life-changing for sure.

There was one teacher everyone feared: Clayton Burroughs. We feared him because he held kids accountable, he meant business, and he made you understand the importance of education even though at that time, fun for us was more important.

A prominent black male, he stood about six feet tall, sported a head full of hair, cut low, and had a smile that filled the entire school when he walked around.

If you were selected to have Mr. Burroughs as your teacher, not only was it an honor, but it was time to grow up quick, and I knew this. With his reputation for grooming all of his students to be successful, I had to be ready for lessons on top of what my parents taught me: the likes of clean clothes every day, wearing a tie on occasion, no joking around, doing chores at home. Lots of things I was ready for at home, but not during school. However, the choice wasn't mine. The older kids that had him the year before told us horror stories, great stories, and what it was like being a student of his. All I remembered were the horror stories, and I was praying that I didn't get him as my teacher. I wanted the easy way out, so to speak.

It was the summer of June 1976. I'll remember one impactful day for the rest of my life, for it made me who I am today, and I continue to use it as a standard by which I live. Even though I've forgotten its importance at times, it's stayed with me. For almost all of the kids in East Cleveland, those who attended Chambers Elementary School and graduated from the sixth grade, this was the hallmark of our success. It was a special day, meaningful, and known as our *commencement*. I was told back then that *commencement* meant *to start—to start your life*. I completed the fifth grade, and later that summer, I would get the news. For me, it seemed like bad news at the time.

I remember my sister calling to me while I was outside playing. "Doubleo, Mommy just told me that Mr. Burroughs is going to be your teacher. Aren't you happy?"

"Hell, nah," I countered. "Don't you know how mean Mr. Burroughs is?" It seemed like my summer ended right there. The pressure had already started building, and I felt like I wanted to pee my pants. My sister could see the look on my face. I was shaken to my core.

"Boy, you'll be fine. You might as well get ready. Mommy loves Mr. Burroughs. All the parents do."

"Yeah, I know," I replied, "but the kids don't. You see the stress on their faces when they leave school, right?"

"No, I don't. They look happy and mature to me."

"Shoot, I'm not ready for this." My shoulders slumped, and I went into the house to pee. Her news brought that on.

The summer passed, and I started my sixth grade year.

Mr. Burroughs was the man who told me what commencement meant, and although as young as I was, what it took to move forward, and in most ways, what lay ahead for me. I was terrified of leaving the sixth grade, of leaving his grasp on me. Would I ever see him again? Would I be able to hold on to what he taught me? Those were my thoughts. I had no answers, but more importantly, I had the lessons he taught me buried deep in my soul.

Mr. Burroughs was intense. He walked with a confident strut and drove a green Mercury that had a beige top. There were times when I would sneak a peak before school in the parking lot where the teachers parked, just to see if he was absent on school days. He never was. I'd also watch his car leave the parking lot at the end of the school day, just to make sure he was gone for the day and not coming back. My thinking was, *I need a break*, but that break never came, and I'm thankful for it. His everyday presence with us would be instrumental for a lifetime, and that's why I am who I am today.

He always dressed in slacks, button-down shirts, leather belts, and clean, polished shoes. He got on us about missing belts or missing belt loops, and keeping our shirts tucked in. I hated the feeling of a tucked-in shirt, but that thought quickly left my mind when I entered Mr. Burroughs's sixth grade classroom.

One of his signature traits was his laugh, a laugh that would make you laugh just from hearing it. Sometimes, though, that laugh meant trouble. It could be sarcastic just as well, and I knew the difference, depending on what I did, right or wrong.

Mr. Burroughs was well-known throughout the school district for being a great teacher, strict when he needed to be, and one who didn't play. However, he took really good care of us. He was by far the best teacher in Ohio, probably the best teacher in the world, by my account, and others would easily agree.

He took great care of us, but at the same time, if we got out of line, there was hell to pay. Mr. Burroughs had many ways to get my attention. His voice was never loud, but it was stern, kind of low and slow when he wanted to get your attention, like a powerful growl. You could feel his words enter your soul.

Sometimes his voice was bone-chilling, and when this happened, I would stop in my tracks and stare directly at him, hoping for mercy. Most times, if not all, we knew when he was upset. His words would slowly come out of his mouth, as if in slow motion. When that happened, you could almost see the words slowly rolling off his tongue, like little balls of fire.

"Mr. Walker," he would say, "you owe me, young man. Gimme five."

"Gimme five" meant five swats on the buttocks, and I saw the words *gimme five* clear as day, floating in the air. Swatting was held in the coatroom, back where the other classmates couldn't see you. It was scary to watch other kids walk back there, knowing what was about to happen, but what was even scarier was having to walk back there yourself.

The coatroom was about five to eight feet from my desk, but walking back there in slow motion made it seem like a mile long. By the time I got back there, my palms were sweaty, my face was dripping with sweat, and my butt cheeks were already tight. I would then enter the coatroom, hearing Mr. Burroughs's voice the entire time as he sat at his desk, calling out directions and what to do when you got back there, not that I needed any direction. He knew that hearing his voice the whole time during the transition made it worse.

"When you get back there, Mr. Walker, get ready. Don't make me wait on you," he would bark out.

For some reason, it seemed that each time I got into trouble I was wearing rough, stiff, Levi jeans, and the material wasn't a safe haven at all. In fact, the sting from the swats lasted longer in that material, and it felt like my butt was on fire all the way down to my feet.

The only thing worse than getting swatted was waiting on him. The entire classroom was in silence as he approached, so it was just he and I. I knew he was getting closer by the creaking of the floor. With every step he took, I knew where he was. That was just as painful as getting my swats. He made it painfully calculating.

When Mr. Burroughs arrived in the coatroom, he had his bottom lip curled in. "Y'all gonna learn one day," he said.

I knew then it was serious business.

He adjusted my pants to get that certain tightness for the maximum impact, and it worked every time.

Here comes the swing of a lifetime, I thought.

My hands perched on the coat hooks, head straight ahead, I heard him say, "Don't look at me, Mr. Walker. Look straight ahead."

His saying "Mr. Walker" surely didn't make me feel any better. In fact, for some reason, it made me feel worse, as if I was an older kid getting punished for doing what little kids do. Looking back at him before being swatted was my way of doing two things: asking for mercy and trying to make him feel sorry for me. Neither worked, so on with the pain. On those days, it felt like I was going to pee my pants, but I never did. That surely might have helped make him feel bad, but it seemed like the pee didn't want to come out, like it was scared to. I was on my own for sure, no liquids to spare or surrender, just my little eleven-year-old butt cheeks.

I turned around in anticipation of the pain. Why I did this each time, I have no clue because in doing so, all I could see was how high he raised the paddle and the manner in which it was coming down to destroy my butt. He always swung hard, with an upward, curving motion. This motion made sure he got the entire butt cheek. Bottom lip still tucked in, he used his other hand to pull tightly on my Levi jeans for maximum impact.

Swack, swack, swack, swack, swack. He paused three to five seconds between each swing so the stinging would settle in. I felt all five. I knew Mr. Burroughs didn't like doing this, but he sure got his point across.

This happened quite often when our class went on field trips. My friends and I never paid attention to the orator at the Cleveland Museum of Natural History, the Cleveland Museum of Art, or anywhere else we went for a class field trip. The threat of the paddle surely captured our attention.

Speaking of paddles, Mr. Burroughs kept a couple of paddles in his drawer, and I specifically remember the names of them: the Equalizer and the Motivator. I had the opportunity to get to know both of them. Back then, I didn't know what the Motivator was. I didn't care, either. I just knew that I didn't want that thing hitting my ass. I learned pretty quick what it meant to be motivated—motivated to stay out of trouble, not because of the swats, but because Mr. Burroughs motivated me forever.

Hitting my ass a few times throughout the year happened quite often, painful days for me and one special group of male classmates. Back then teachers were authorized to use a paddle, so it wasn't a big deal if they did. For the most part, there was a group of us, more like five of us, who constantly got into trouble. We got swatted, and just generally broke the rules. We were either mannish, dangerous, or simply looking for fun. I suppose we all needed some sort of an outlet. Who knows why we did what we did, but it was fun, probably because we liked living on the edge, and it felt good.

Danger excited all of us. I'm not sure why, but it did, and we all had a good upbringing. I never understood why we wanted to rob a train, but we did.

* * *

It was the fall of 1976, and we were sitting on a hilltop. Rain was lightly coming down, and the morning dew was sinking into our pants, but we were chillin': me, Jerry, George, and one other.

Jerry was tall for his age, about five feet eight inches, and weighed about 160 pounds. He had a big, puffy, orange Afro, a rather muscular frame, and light skin. The girls liked him, and my sister was crazy about him.

George was skinny, about the same height as Jerry, with brown skin, straight white teeth, and black hair. He had by far the worst hair I'd ever seen on any human being, but you couldn't tell him any different. His hair on top was straightened with a hot comb, by his mother. There were times I'd go over to his house, and from the front door, I could see heavy, thick smoke floating in the kitchen. I thought to myself, *Is there a fire in there?* I soon found out.

One day, I rang the doorbell a few times. No one answered, so I peeped in the window. I couldn't see anything, but all of a sudden, I heard, "Boy, get yo nappy-headed ass in here."

Jerry walked into the kitchen nice and slow.

I pulled back from the window, chuckling. "Damn," I said to myself, "that's where the smoke is coming from."

Jerry was standing in front of the stove, his mother behind him, and she was dragging that hot comb through the top of his head. She never touched the sides. That part of his hair stayed nappy as hell. The hot comb would sit on the stove until it turned orange, then she'd pull it through his hair again, his head tilting back. She repeated this several times. You could actually hear his hair frying, as if it was being cooked in hot grease.

"Come in, li'l boy," his mom said.

I walked in, terrified, and sat there and watched as George wiggled in pain. Sometimes, she burned the tips of his ears. His hair was full of grease, Sulfur 8 grease. He looked like he had come right out of the 1950s. Most times he would scream like Malcolm X did in the movie when his friend put that cream in his hair. That was how George sounded when that hot comb went through his hair, touching his scalp.

When she was done, he looked in the mirror. "Dub, you like this?" he asked me.

"Nah, man, I really don't," I said, frowning. "You look older. You look like a broke pimp . . . and your hair stinks. It smells like burnt bacon." I had other questions for him. "George, is she your real mom? She's dark as hell, and you're brown-skinned. She's thick, and you're very thin. Dude, what's up?"

"Why you ask me that, man? Not funny, man, not funny at all." He turned to his mother. "Hey, Ma, can you do Doubleo's . . ."?

Before he could finish his sentence, I was out the front door. George lied all the time, but he was a cool dude. He was adopted.

*　*　*

We were in East Cleveland, on Shaw Avenue, right next to a bridge, one that supported train tracks. You could feel the vibration of the train coming from miles away. We were flicking blades of grass, swatting bees and flies, lying in the grass, legs perched up, elbows behind us, waiting anxiously for a chance to steal something, anything. A group of us, about five, had nothing better to do, so we decided to head to the bridge.

Jerry, our fearless leader, said, "Dub, what are we going to get today, man?"

"Shoot, I don't know, man. Anything."

We laughed hysterically.

The train was slowly coming down the tracks. It was about a mile or two away.

Jerry said, "Yo, Dub, you hear that, man?"

"Hell, yeah, and I see it, too."

"I hope it stops here today," Jerry said.

"Yeah, me, too," I replied.

We high-fived and laughed again. When you hear the warning horn, that means to clear the train tracks, but we ignored that warning, hoping the train would stop right where we were. Normally it did, and today wouldn't be any different. We had a plan. My little group and I were all in the sixth grade. A few older guys had joined us.

"Hey, check this out," Jerry said. "Here's the plan, man. Once the train stops, start unlocking the boxcars, and we'll set up an assembly line to get what we want."

"Cool," George said. "I'm in, too, man."

"To be honest," I said, "I hope it has some TVs on it. I'm tired of that damn small TV with hangers and aluminum foil hanging off the back. No reception most days. I hate that."

"Yeah, and when you touch it, you get shocked."

"Y'all silly, man, but yeah, we all got those in the crib," Jerry said.

The train arrived with a loud hissing noise. We knew then it was time to get our goods, and we knew then the train wasn't going anywhere for a while.

"George," Jerry called out, "unlock the damn boxcar. Quit being scared, man."

"I ain't scared."

"I told you, I want some TVs," I said. "We make our line after George opens the boxcar, and we hop in. Help me, Jerry. I can't get up there."

"Okay, man, watch out. Let me do it." Jerry climbed in. "Damn, man, look at those nice shoes."

"What kind are they?" we asked.

"Turf shoes," he replied. "A lot of them. We hit the jackpot."

Back then, turf shoes were a hot commodity and very expensive, too. The NFL players all wore them. We talked and laughed after unloading boxes of Astroturf tennis shoes from the train. These shoes were quite popular in the '70s. The older guys with us took most of the shoes and gave us each a pair to wear or sell. Ron-Ron, a tall, roundheaded dude with white teeth, a wide smile, and an athletic build, had taken charge, and we knew it.

Mark, Ron-Ron's friend, was his backup. Mark was a great football player, very authoritative, with muscles everywhere. They looked out for us, but would beat our ass if we told anyone about what we were doing or didn't listen to their orders. They were both about seven years older than us.

For some reason, the train would always stop on this bridge, and each time, we would time it just right.

"Hey, hey," a man called out. "Get your ass out of there."

I looked at Jerry, eyes wide open.

He told George and everyone else to just run. "Go, go, go, man. Let's go. Run! Don't leave shit behind, boy."

We all jumped down the hill, fell, and rolled the rest of the way down, laughing the whole time.

The conductor from the train, a white guy, ran down the tracks. I could hear him breathing hard, stumbling across the tracks. "Bring back my shit," he yelled. "I'm gonna tell the police on ya, you just wait."

We ran just a little ways away where we could see him head back to the train. Once he did that, we went back up the hill to get more merchandise. We knew when he was ready to take off again, the train would make a loud snap between boxcars. That was our clue to stand clear.

The train left, and we had lots of shoes to keep and sell—or we would have if the older guys hadn't taken almost everything.

That was a hard day's work, so we developed a pretty huge appetite. Our minds still racing, blood still pumping, there was more mischief to get into. We decided to head to the nearest grocery store to steal snacks.

Jerry, my close friend, was pretty much our leader when the older guys weren't around. Jerry had a good upbringing, just like most of us, and his mother didn't play. As odd as it may seem, none of our parents were pushovers. We were just devilish and always needed something to get into.

"Yo, man, y'all hungry?" Jerry asked.

"Hell, yeah, man, we're starving," we all responded. "Let's head to Bi-rite's."

Bi-rite's was the nearest grocery store, where we made money carrying groceries for the elderly, and where we turned in empty glass bottles to earn ten cents per bottle for some extra cash. This day, the store was slow. There weren't many people shopping that morning, so we had to make our own way to get food, especially since the older guys hadn't left us much to sell or given us any money. Jerry's plan was simple. We would enter the store, gather a bunch of snacks, candy, and juice, stuff everything under our coats, and make it out of the store without being caught.

Regardless of whether we were in or out of school, Mr. Burroughs had a way of keeping an eye on us. Nevertheless, we took a chance on him finding us out. We were starving.

Jerry gave us all guidance as to which aisle to go to, what to steal, when to get the hell out of there, and where to meet up when we were done. My heart was racing, and we were smiling, nervous, and ready to stuff our coats. We were pumped.

After our coats were stuffed, Jerry gave us the eye to leave, and we exited. As we left the store, we ran into Daria. Daria and her sisters were all very pretty, from a beautiful family. Her mother was pretty, too, and I had an attraction to her as well. I remember approaching Daria with our nice goodies, feeling happy-go-lucky, and not wanting to share. Daria asked how we got those things.

I easily lied. "We carried groceries for the older ladies in Bi-Rite."

Of course, Daria knew right away that I was lying, and she was also mad that we didn't share our treats with her. As any jealous kid would do, she told on us.

Her telling on us set our minds to thinking about the punishment we were going to receive. We already knew what it was. Man, was Jerry pissed about that! When we got to school that fall, Mr. Burroughs knew about what had gone down, and there was hell to pay. He lined all five of us up, took us to the coatroom, and lit into our butts. Each one of us took five major swats on the butt, and you could tell how painful it was because as Mr. Burroughs swung and hit each kid, the one who was next in line would piss himself out of fear. Just imagine how you would feel knowing that you were next. That was an unforgettable punishment, for sure.

Despite the paddling, we never hated Mr. Burroughs. He loved us to death, and we loved him right back. He gave all of us extraordinary life lessons that are still with us today. Out of all the kids he taught, he had some wonderful kids do some astonishing things—in no small part due to the sense of worth and discipline that he instilled in each of us. All-American basketball players, NBA players, lawyers, doctors, musicians, successful military careers, and a host of other prominent leaders in the world came out of his classroom at Chambers Elementary School.

Looking back on it now, I really appreciate the type of teacher he was. Even at the young age of eleven, we knew we had the coolest, smartest, wittiest, most caring and passionate teacher in the world. Mr. Burroughs was one hell of a man and teacher, and to this day, because of him, I speak the way I do, I write the way I do, and I remain fully aware of my grammar, punctuation, spelling, and complete sentences because of him. There are many more gifts that he has given thousands of kids, of course. Those were just to name a few. Because of him, I also pay attention to my belt and belt loops and tuck my shirt in. I'm thankful that in June of 1976, I was notified that Mr. Burroughs would be my sixth grade teacher. That day changed my life forever.

Sixth grade was a special time in my life, for sure. At Chambers Elementary School, being in the sixth grade came with an honor. You felt accomplished, smart, excited, and ready for the world. The school officials created a thing called "Clap Out." Clap Out was a big thing for sixth graders at Chambers. On that day, everyone dressed up in their best outfit, and the fifth graders and below aligned the hallways, clapping us out as we exited the school. This was an amazing moment for all sixth graders. We were considered graduates, and the school made sure we felt it. Even now, talking about it, I get chills. Clap Out was a thing to remember.

When you left the school on Clap Out day, family awaited you outside, giving you kisses, hugs, handshakes, cards, gifts, balloons, and all types of tokens and memorabilia. I loved it and hated it, all at the same time. I hated it because my family wasn't there, except for my sister because she was a fifth grader and she was next. My parents had divorced, my mother was broke, and I didn't receive any gifts, tokens, hugs, kisses, balloons, or anything of the sort. I was pissed, hurt, mad, and lonely—and it was about to get worse.

I walked home alone that day after Clap Out, going past all of the happy families. I ran into J's mother, and she decided to do something nice and take us all to Bob's Big Boy. I dug into a hamburger, fries, and a thick milkshake—still broke, but feeling better on a full stomach. But all good things must come to an end. I had to go home, back to the little house of horrors.

By this time, it was getting late, and Jerry's mother dropped me off. "Doubleo," she said, "is anyone home?"

"Sure," I replied.

"But it's dark in the house," she said.

"I know. We don't have any electricity."

She offered to have me come to their house, but I knew that my mother wouldn't like it, so I declined. As bad as I wanted to go with J, his mom, and his little sister, I had to go home— home to a dark, dirty, half-empty house. It sucked, and I hated it. My father was gone, the divorce was in full swing, we were poor, and things were getting worse. What could I do? I was an angry little kid, a lost soul, lifeless.

CHAPTER 17
Pissy Sleepwalker

I destroyed my mattress

My new bed

You can't help someone with the wrong mental attitude,
but you can't stop someone with the right mental attitude.

IN JUNE 1976, I would be exposed to all of my friends. Our house was full of animosity, mostly because of the violent fights. Paired with our low income, life was just downright hard. Don't get me wrong. We shared some great times together, my family and I, but for the most part, I was extremely overwhelmed with dysfunction. No matter what, though, I was still functioning.

I believe I turned into a bed wetter from living in a constant state of fear, always terrified before going to bed. It wasn't that I was full of water, juice, or Kool-Aid. I went to bed every night scared of waking up to my parents' fighting and having no control over it. In addition to this, I was also a sleepwalker for many years. My siblings thought this was hilarious, and at some point, I did, too. I had to laugh about it with them, just to keep from crying.

I had all sorts of issues, but I managed to overcome them all in due time. I pissed the bed from kindergarten up until the sixth grade, and I had no way of controlling it. The tragic events in my life not only affected my sleeping habits, but I also sucked my thumb for years. I had a number of childhood habits like these that developed as ways to soothe my pain and make me feel comfortable from within. I blame sucking my thumb for the overbite and big front teeth that I have today.

Each summer the students at Chambers Elementary School took a one-week-long trip to Red Raider Camp. The camp was fun and full of events.

I had been trying my hardest not to pee in bed. I didn't drink water before I went to sleep, I used the bathroom before bedtime—I tried it all. Nothing worked. I knew that peeing the bed at camp would be mortifying, and I wasn't ready for that. Sure enough, that first night at camp, I wet the bed. Then the second. Then the third. I wet the bed every night that week, and you could smell it.

I thought that no one knew until Randy, my camp counselor, came to my bed, handed me some plastic sheets, and walked away. A cool white guy, Randy was caring, compassionate, and helpful. He told the other counselors after the second night, and they asked me if I was okay.

"Of course not," I told them. "I have nightmares of my parents' fighting."

All they could do as counselors was to talk to me about it. But as hard as they tried to help me, it didn't do any good. The bed-wetting persisted.

That was my first time talking to a counselor about my family troubles, and it felt good to know that someone was concerned, though it didn't solve my problems.

The next counseling that I received was after I was married. That didn't work, either. I had gone almost twenty years without any kind of therapy, intervention, or help with my mental state. I had survived mental torture but had never done anything about it.

When that week of camp was over, we headed home. I had really enjoyed myself, but I felt like a failure for having continued to piss the bed even when I was there. Back at home, things weren't any better. I continued to piss the bed so much that eventually my mother made me sleep on a rug on the floor, as I had destroyed numerous mattresses.

I shared a bunk bed with my brother for some time—the top bunk was mine—but I pissed so much that it would leak down onto his bed. The move from the bed to the floor didn't make it better, for me anyway, because the floor was hard and cold, and there were roaches there, as well. As I slept on the small little rug that became my bed, I pissed so much that it stuck to the floor. The bottom of the mat was a black spongy material, nothing that would withstand my piss, so it soaked it up and literally became part of the floor. My father had to cut the rug from the floor, and upon taking the rug up, we noticed that the floor had become a different color, darkening from beige to yellow, like the color of piss. My bed-wetting went on for years, and I just couldn't seem to control it.

My issues with bed-wetting were just one of many memories that stick out in my mind from the years we spent living at 14408 Alder Avenue. Those years were good, bad, serious, fun, turbulent, off-balance, draining, scary, and tumultuous—to say the least. We were all deeply affected by those events and that house. Still, even though I lived in that totally dysfunctional household, it's important to say that not everything was bad all the time. We knew laughter and fun, and as I've mentioned, one thing that we always got a good laugh over was my sleepwalking.

One night I woke up and found myself standing in the front lawn. I could feel the cool grass, wet with dew, beneath my bare feet. My sister and brother were standing beside me, one on each arm, and giggling like two schoolchildren who'd just been caught pulling off a good prank.

I shook my head, embarrassed. "It happened again, didn't it?"

My sister's face was a dark silhouette against the streetlamp behind her. "It sure did. And it was hilarious."

I felt my shoulders slump in resignation. "What'd I do?"

My brother took over the narrative. "First, you went to the kitchen and kept trying to get into the refrigerator, but you didn't know how to grab the handle. Then you walked up and down the stairs a bunch of times. Then we followed you out here. You were mumbling something about it being time to go to school."

"Why didn't you wake me?" I asked, frustrated that they found the whole thing so amusing.

"Because," my sister said, "it's more fun to see what you're going to do next."

"Ha-ha," I said and turned toward the front porch. "I'm going back to bed."

Sleepwalking can be dangerous, and every time I did it, I was at risk. I joke about it, but now I know that I definitely had some sort of issue or disability. Today, it's something that people have treated medically. Back then, though, my family and I just had no idea what was going on.

CHAPTER 18

Breakthrough—
Broken Up

I WAS ALWAYS ANGRY and had become a dangerous little kid. My mind was all over the place, and I needed something to do, something physical. I decided to play football. We played in the streets with kids in the area and against people in the neighborhood, and I loved it. Football was my favorite sport at the time.

The local football team was very good. They were called the East Cleveland Chiefs, a dominant team and known throughout both the state of Ohio and the rest of the country. Unfortunately, my time with that team was cut short, as my mother had to work at the local bar and often couldn't take me to the practices.

Me quitting the team didn't hurt them at all. They had a pool of kids to pick from, and almost all of them were great athletes from about seven through fourteen years old.

I was pissed, and again, I had to find something to do. There was another team in the area called the Academs. This team had been around just as long as the East Cleveland Chiefs, but they weren't as good. I played for them for one season but didn't have much support getting to practice, and no one ever came to watch me play, so my motivation died out. I left that team as well.

These experiences transformed me. I didn't like being someone who started something and didn't finish it. That lesson would stay with me for the rest of my life, even now when I'm over fifty. Now, once I start something, I have to take it to the end. Learning this was very beneficial to me in life as well, and definitely later on in my future career. Success was inevitable with this type of mind-set, and I learned it, lived it, and loved it. Anyone can adopt this way of thinking, and it works with everything that you do.

But back to my youth football career. I'd already quit twice, and I didn't want to be a quitter anymore. That was when Mr. Sway, who stood about five feet eleven inches tall and weighed about 170 pounds, came driving down our street. He sported a thick mustache and a small Afro of black hair. A really cool man and such a smooth talker, he always wore the best clothes and drove classy cars. Stacy Adam shoes adorned his feet, clean slacks fitted his thin but strong frame, and a freshly ironed shirt with a starched collar wrapped his torso. You could smell his cologne before he got close to you.

Looking at him, I wanted to *be* him, and I was sucked into his conversation immediately. He could get people to do anything. He wore a crooked smile, like a smirk, that made you just want to bust your ass working for him from the instant you met him. He had a way of talking to me that made me feel ten feet tall. Mr. Sway had started another team in the area called the Alcoa Pruitts, named after the famous Cleveland Browns player Greg Pruitt. Never mind that we never saw him, though that would have been nice, as we were all crazy about our Cleveland Browns.

We were playing football in the street one day when my friend Sam said, "Yo, Doubleo, they're looking for players in the area."

"Players?" I said. "What are you talking 'bout?"

"This dude just came down the street looking for kids to play football on a new team. You wanna play?"

"Hell, yeah, I do! Where do we go?"

A few minutes later, Mr. Sway and his coaches came down Alder Avenue. "Hey, young man, I hear you can play football," Mr. Sway said after approaching me.

"Yep," I replied. "We can *all* play. Sure can."

He looked me over while chewing his gum. "Okay. Talk to a few of your friends and come to the field. We'll be waiting over on Woolworth. See you soon."

We all jumped for joy.

He gave me a nod, with his arms crossed, still chewing his gum and wearing that crooked smile.

The other teams in the area had all pretty much already formed up, and we had been left out. This was a breakthrough for us, and it gave a lot of other kids something to do. As for me, I now belonged to a team. I felt a sense of accomplishment, I felt important, and I would not blow this chance.

Mr. Sway formed this team with the local kids, and the coaches were some of the local adults. In the beginning, we didn't have any uniforms, so we were asked to buy our own jerseys to start off with. Our team was formed as best we could, and then the season started. Practices were fun, hard, and a bit rough because we didn't have the best equipment, but we made it happen.

Our leading coach was a guy named Brocky. About six feet four and 250 pounds, he was a pretty nice guy until you pissed him off. Even though he was twice our size, he wouldn't hesitate to slap the shit out of us through our helmets. This happened to quite a few players on the team, but not to me. I was very good at football. I could run fast, and I loved hitting other kids extremely hard. Suffering from the divorce of my parents, I took my anger out on other kids during the game and even my teammates during practice. I loved it. I would hit them so hard, my entire body would hurt later on, and my head would hurt for days. Headaches became the norm for me, as did hurting other kids.

I miss Mr. Sway so much. He passed away some years back, but he gave us the opportunity of a lifetime, took care of hundreds of people all over Cleveland, and gave people jobs and careers. He helped save a lot of kids' lives—mine, specifically.

Football consumed me. I loved the excitement, but I really loved the way that I could destroy a young kid's body by exploding into his soul. I was short at that age, but I was also very thick and strong, which aided me in overcoming my short stature.

Our first season as the Alcoa Pruitts was horrible, to say the least, but we had fun. I made a lot of tackles throughout the season, ran the football often, and was invited to the All-Star game. I never went, because my mother couldn't afford it.

Still, I enjoyed the feeling of success. The highlight of our season was when I caught a ten-yard pass and ran about ninety yards for a touchdown. What a great feeling, and best of all, my father was there to witness it. I could see the honor and happiness in his eyes, the jubilation, and how proud he was of me.

Mr. Sway was also proud of me that day. Even though we lost the game by a lot, the referee tried to take our touchdown away, until Mr. Sway had words with him. "Come on, man, you gonna take that away from us?" he yelled at the referee. "You gotta be kidding me."

"Yep, sure I am," the referee said.

"What, you serious?" Mr. Sway yelled. "I don't think so. One way or the other, we keepin' that touchdown. You don't take things from these kids, not my kids."

And we kept the touchdown. It might not have been much to many people, but it was special to me.

I missed my father dearly, and I couldn't wait to see him at each game or when it was my time to visit him. These thoughts never went away. Each practice would end with Coach Brocky talking to us and Mr. Sway giving us hope. Never mind that we lost every game except one. They told us to just have fun, and even though we were nowhere close to the best in the league, we had by far the best banquet.

Our end-of-season celebration was held in a very lavish hotel—I think it was the Bond Court in Cleveland, maybe downtown—and we were allowed to spend the night. For the night's events, my father took me to get a suit at the Giant Tiger, a store that's now closed. I bought a three-piece powder-blue suit, with a tie and black shoes. Looking back on it now, I realize that suit was ugly as hell.

Mr. Sway had his shit together even back then. He was a manager, proprietor, husband, father, and a businessman well-known throughout Ohio for his hair care products, the Jheri curl. Our banquet was the best around, a wonderful night, and I ended up with the Most Outstanding Player trophy, another proud moment for my father and me. Mr. Sway brought us all together, and taught us at an early age what a team was all about. The night of the banquet, all of these pieces came together.

The night ended, and it was time to go back to my mother's house, something that I dreaded because it was just awful there after the divorce. Coming home to no lights, no water, and at times, no heat was a bitch. I could easily go a week without having breakfast, changing my clothes, or having a shower. Don't get me wrong. My mother did her best, but sometimes that didn't even help. Most days, coming home from football practice, I had no clue if the electricity was on or off until either I'd reach to hit the light switch, and nothing happened, or my sister would tell me.

"Toni, what's up?" I asked. "Did you eat yet?"

"Nah, whatever's in the refrigerator is spoiled. The electricity's off, so don't eat anything in there."

"Where are you?" I asked.

"Over here."

"Oh, shoot, I didn't see you." I hated talking to my sister in the dark.

There were plenty of times we had to borrow water from the neighbors' faucet in back of their house. Because the water was cold, we had to use hot plates to warm it up, and we used the hot plates to cook with as well. I hated living like that, and I made a solemn vow to myself that when I got older, I would never ever live like that or allow my kids to live that way.

One day after football practice, I came home and there was an orange extension cord going from our house to the neighbors' house. We were using their electricity. Living in poverty wasn't just uncomfortable. It was embarrassing, to say the least.

Our phone was shut off, too. The clothes I wore to school were torn, old, and missing zippers. It was horrible. My coats were ripped and buttons were missing. It was hell. There were times that I'd wake up and realize that all of my underclothes were dirty.

One day, after waking up late, I rushed downstairs into the basement to find some clean underwear. I saw a white pair that looked pretty fresh, even though they weren't. I put them on, anyway. I noticed that they seemed a bit larger than my normal underwear, but I didn't think anything of it. I figured they belonged to my brother. Well, I went off to school, and ironically it turned out that day that I had a headache and had to go and see the school nurse. Sitting there in her office, I was twitching and moving around quite a bit.

"Sit still," she told me.

"I can't!" I said. "My butt is itching."

She asked me why, and I told her about how I had been rushing and put on my brother's dirty underwear by mistake.

She took a look and said, "Little boy, you have on your mother's girdle."

I wore my mother's girdle to school that day. How embarrassing that was. No one knew but the nurse and me, and she promised not to tell anyone. She told me just to take it off when I got home.

I gave her a sheepish look, put my head down, and left her office.

Food was scarce, as well. Going to school early in the morning hungry was a bitch, so I had to do what I had to do. There was a kid named Charles in my class, always well-dressed, clean-cut, well-mannered, and very nerdy. We'd sit together for lunch each day, and I'd watch him at lunchtime. His parents would make him nice sandwiches that looked delicious, and he'd never share. Actually, he didn't have to. One day, I got tired of being hungry and asked him for a piece of his sandwich. Of course, he told me no. I was hungry and pissed, and I knew there was nothing he could or would do if I took his food. He had some very tasty-looking Rice Krispie treats, pretty large, too. Once I saw that, I got angry and snatched one right from his hands as he prepared his mouth to devour it. I took his lunch and ate it all. He told my teacher. I got five swats that day but didn't care because my belly was finally full. Charles never sat next to me again during lunch.

All of the house parties were over. Sheila moved out of the

neighborhood, so no more threesomes, which was a good thing. With my father being gone, we had no manly figure in the house, just my brother, and he was about seven years older than I was. We had the same mother, but different fathers. His father never came by to visit him. I wouldn't meet him until later in life, and I didn't care to meet him, either.

CHAPTER 19

My Gay Mentor

IN THE FALL of 1978, I met my first mentor, Chaz. He was gay.

Lots happened that year, for sure.

It was misty outside, with a light drizzle of rain. My mother was working at another bar, still serving drinks, meeting people, and enjoying what she did. I was at home, playing and looking out of the window, waiting for her to come home. Normally, when she came home from the bar, she'd bring snacks, sandwiches, and some juice. Working there helped her make ends meet as best as she could.

My mother possessed an uncanny ability to meet, not strange people, but I'd say, different people. Most were cool and some were a bit quirky, but I can honestly admit that they were all very intelligent. On occasion, I would meet them, too. Seeing as though my mother was quite cerebral herself, I'm sure she attracted those types—mainly men. After all, she was very attractive.

I'm the same way when it comes to meeting people. I'm drawn to people who think differently, too. At times, mostly on Saturdays, I'd work with my mother at the corner bar, cleaning up, washing dishes, and cutting the grass. On one particular Saturday, there was a gentleman I found unique. He treated my mother with respect. I truly enjoyed that, and I was no longer fearing for my mother's life when this man came around, or when he was at the bar with her. I didn't know why, but he never flirted with my mother, at least, not around me.

My father had moved out, and I was craving a male figure in my life. What I didn't know was that my prayer would be answered when I was twelve, almost thirteen. I knew a lot about little girls my age by then, and I knew a few things about older women, but I still knew very little about myself. That would soon change when a male role model finally came into my life. He moved in with us in 1978. This would become an integral part of my growth. That was when I met Chaz.

Chaz came into our life, and things seemed to get better for me, at least from an educational standpoint. When my mother introduced us to him, my first instinct was to wonder what my father would think about a gay man living with us.

My sister hissed at me. "Psssst, Doubleo, come here."

"Yeah, what's up?" I asked her.

"Is he gay?" she whispered.

"I don't know, but his shorts are surely tight."

We both laughed hysterically, leaning back and holding our stomachs.

My brother seemed pretty moved by the thought that Chaz might be gay. "Did you see the way he walks?" he asked me.

"Yes, I saw that. He seems to swish a little."

Chaz moved in that fall. We made room for him, but we were a bit hesitant at first. Even though my father was gone, I still held him in high regard. The way we were raised, we never made assumptions about anyone. We merely accepted people as they were, and I'm still this way today. My sister didn't have a problem with Chaz, either. As a matter of fact, Chaz and my sister got along great. After moving in, he quickly became acclimated to our family ways. We were all pretty open people, so it was easy for him to get along with us.

He always wore tight little jeans that were rolled up at the knee area and cutoff shorts, and he pranced around the house, gay and proud as could be. He often wore a tight white T-shirt. It was so tight that you could see his nipples and chest hair protruding through the shirt.

Mr. Chaz, if not gay, would have made any woman happy. He was friendly, free-spirited, intelligent, caring, and passionate. He just didn't want a woman. He became my friend and mentor.

As a friend, he loved my mother very much, and he was very good for her. Even though he was gay, someone who loved and dated men, he actually taught me a lot about how to be a man. He knew exactly how a man should look, think, and act, and also how to be attractive to women. Even though he felt no romantic interest in women, he had a woman's perspective, so it made sense to me to listen to him. He knew what he liked in men, just like a woman.

My older brother stayed away from Chaz, and I understood, but I thought it was rude. Chaz did have some effeminate characteristics, but he knew what the hell he was talking about, and I wanted that guidance. My father was one hell of a man, but living down on Hough, he was about thirty minutes away. He was still working full time at Ford, so my time with him was limited to the weekends. I felt comfortable around Chaz, and I would talk to him about everything.

Chaz and my mother smoked a lot of marijuana, laughed all the time, talked about worldly issues, and got along great. It was refreshing to have some semblance of peace in our home, and things were getting better, so much better that Chaz started to ask me daily how I was doing in school. I explained to him how tough my sixth grade teacher was, that we feared him but also loved him, and about how he made us learn and grow at the same time. I also shared with him some of my deepest secrets about how I was feeling sexually. I told him what I had been going through with the threesome, molestation, porn, and being poor. Then I told him that I was experiencing withdrawal from not seeing Sheila, porn, and the older ladies around the house. I needed an outlet, and I needed to release.

Chaz talked to me about life, school, my friends, and a host of other things. We discussed everything. He literally made me smarter. Going through what I had gone through, I didn't understand why Chaz liked men when it seemed that he could have any woman that he wanted. He educated me on his lifestyle, how he believed it began for him, as far as being gay, and how he eventually came out of the closet.

"Chaz," I asked him, "What do you like about men, and what do you not like about women?"

"Hand me that lighter. I need a cigarette for this one." Chaz lit up his cigarette, took a drag, inhaled deeply, and leaned his head back and blew the smoke in the air. "First off, I think titties are gross. They just look like they're not supposed to be there. I like seeing a man's chest."

I waved the smoke out of my face and rested my hand on his shoulder. "Please don't say anything, but I like titties. I think they look great on women, like they are *supposed* to be there." I chuckled hysterically.

"Well, that's good. I'm glad you do like them, but I don't. I hate them. Let me get back to answering your question. I don't want to talk about titties. There are lots of things that I like about men. What do you want to know?"

"Well, not much, 'cause I'm a bit nervous about hearing what you have to say. But go ahead, tell me anyway."

"Okay, here goes. I see men like women see men. I've tried

to like women, but it just doesn't work for me. It doesn't do anything for me when I think of a woman. I knew I was gay when I was five or six years old."

"No way," I said. "That's impossible. Are you for real? Five or six? So, when you were five or six, what did you feel? How did you know?"

"I knew because I would get excited when my male cousin would come to visit. You know, like I would feel a weird feeling come over me. He wasn't gay or anything, and he didn't know that I liked him, but I did. I felt something with him, and it's called an attraction."

"Wow, so he never knew?"

"No, not at all, and I didn't want anyone else to know, either. It was like my little secret. I felt kind of like a girl when he'd come over. I wanted to play with him, just him and me, and no one else."

"Did you all play, Chaz?"

"Yep, but when we did play, we would wrestle. He was much bigger than I was, so when we'd wrestle around, I knew he would get me down, or get behind me. That's when I knew that I liked him and that I liked men, really. Him being behind me felt like we were going to have sex. At least that's what I was thinking. I'm sure he was just wrestling me and trying to win the match. I wanted him to win, too."

"Ha, ha, ha. You're crazy. Couldn't he tell that you wanted him behind you?"

"No, he had no clue. At first I'd act like I was fighting him, like I wanted to win, but I didn't want to win the match. I just became even more turned on when he'd really try and I'd feel his aggression, like his muscles would flinch. Now, that got me really excited."

"Oh, wow, so I guess you did know, huh?"

"Yeah, but I kind of didn't have a choice, I don't think.

We'd wrestle so much that we'd be sweating. That really turned me on."

"What do you mean you didn't have a choice?"

"Well, you see, my uncle raped me."

"What? How old were you?"

"Well, he started touching me early on. It had to be before I was six."

"Did you tell anyone?"

"No, not at all. I was terrified to tell anyone. I felt like they wouldn't believe me. This is what I remember. One day when I was home alone, he was watching me, and he just started to touch me. He put his hands down my underwear and kissed me all over. Then he raped me, and it hurt bad. It hurt like hell, I swear, and I bled a lot. In a weird way, I felt like he was taking care of me for some odd reason."

I looked at Chaz in amazement. "Wow," I said. "Do you think that you started being gay then, or what?"

"Possibly. That had a lot to do with it, I'm sure."

"Okay, okay. That's horrible, but back to why you like men."

"I told you, you little dummy."

"Ha-ha, Chaz. Okay, yeah, I see now. Okay, one more question."

"Sure, go ahead."

I chuckled and tried to hold it in, but I couldn't even get my question out.

"Go ahead, you little joker," Chaz said as he smoked his cigarette. "Let it out."

"Are you the lady or the man?"

"Ha, I knew you were going to ask me that."

"Well, I mean, how do you know which person you are? I just don't understand."

"Well, I'm not going to get into that. It's much too deep for you right now. I feel you're a bit too young."

"Okay, that's cool. Maybe I don't really want to know, but . . . can I guess?" I looked at him and laughed.

"There you go again with that little laugh, but sure, go ahead."

"Well, when you first moved in, me and Toni kind of thought you were gay. We'd laugh at your tight shorts and tight T-shirt, so I told her you were like a woman."

"Hmmm, well, that's a good thought, and we'll just leave it at that. Maybe one day I'll tell you."

"I think I already know," I told Chaz. "You swish a lot, like a woman." I laughed again and we hugged and went outside.

Chaz put out his cigarette and blew out the remaining smoke. "Don't let the streetlight catch you, you little joker. Hey, Doubleo, guess what?"

"What?" I asked as I ran down the porch stairs and jumped, barely missing the last stair.

"I have a boyfriend," he shouted.

I stopped, turned around, and put my finger up to my mouth. "Shhh, don't say that too loud. My friends are out here. A boyfriend? So that means, if you have a boyfriend, then he has a girlfriend, which means you're the girl. Oops, I mean the woman, right?"

"Go, little boy," Chaz said with a wide smile on his face. "Get your butt outside."

Chaz was a force of stability and peace in my life that I desperately needed. I loved him dearly, gay or not.

* * *

That school year came to an end, and summer vacation was beginning. It was after school and kids were all playing in the street. Nothing ever happened to us there, aside from one of the old neighbors, Mr. Wilson, screaming at us about running on his grass. His lawn was nice, green, and well-manicured, and he didn't like us running through there while we were playing football. Most days, he stopped us by standing out on his lawn with a stick, just waiting for one of us to run by. Some days he was nice, while other days he would wear a scowl waiting for us to just touch his grass. And whenever we ran too close, he whacked us with that stick. Pretty soon, other parents started to follow suit.

So, that's how it usually was when we played outside. Normal stuff. And the kids in our neighborhood, just like most kids anywhere else, loved ice cream. For some reason, on this day in early summer, no one was playing in the street, which seemed odd because that was what we did all the time. I remember hearing music and then seeing that big white truck round the corner. It was the ice cream man. We all jumped for joy and rushed into the street. We stopped the truck and got in line for ice cream. I always wanted to be in front, so I pushed my way up there, bumping kids out of the way, trying to be the first one to get mine before he ran out of treats. I was first in line, but one little girl didn't like that. We argued, she pushed me, and then she tried to run away.

Before I could chase her, she crossed in front of the ice cream truck, and *boom*. A car struck her extremely hard.

I watched in horror as she flew up into the air and then hit the ground. Another *boom*. Her head hit the ground first, then her back, then her legs.

The car careened up onto the neighbors' lawn, one front tire on the lawn and the other three tires in the street.

"Oh my God," shouted the driver as he jumped out, his head bleeding from hitting the windshield. "Is she okay?"

"I don't know," I responded. "Please help us."

We all ran over to find her lying there with her eyes staring straight up into the sky, blood coming from her head and everywhere else. She wasn't making a sound.

The ice cream truck music stopped, the engine stopped, and it became totally quiet. It all seemed to happen in slow motion.

In a loud voice, the ice cream man yelled, "Oh no, help her. God help her. Someone call an ambulance. Please hurry."

The sun was shining, but in my mind, it seemed gloomy. Kids were scattered, crying.

In the chaos, parents were yelling, "Get back, get back. Give her some room."

I could see blood, smashed ice cream, and her feet were as still as the car that hit her.

Her mother came rushing down off her porch. "Sonya!" she yelled. "My baby, my baby." Angrily, she turned to the onlookers. "Y'all get away from her."

I could smell the burnt rubber from the car's screeching tires. I was shocked, terrified, and crying. People were yelling and screaming, pointing at me.

"Doubleo, what did you do?"

I was standing there with my ice cream in my hand. It had started to melt and run down my hand. I looked down at Sonya. Her eyes stared straight to the sky, and she was bleeding from somewhere. No one knew where.

"I didn't do anything," I belted out through my tears, my nose running. I was shaking. I dropped my ice cream and threw my hands to the side. "I swear, I didn't do anything. Leave me alone."

"Yes, you did," another little boy yelled. "You shoved her out of line, punk."

"Shut up, you a punk," I responded.

"Doubleo, why are you so stupid?" her mother said under her breath.

"I didn't mean to do it. I swear I didn't."

It was a horrible day. I didn't make her run into the street. She ran from me because she thought that I was going to hit her. I wasn't. The car that hit her had a dent in it. Her mother was standing there crying, my mother was holding me. It was chaos. I was afraid, and everyone was blaming me. I was only a kid. I didn't know what to do.

The little girl was taken to the hospital with major injuries. I took all the blame from everyone: parents, kids, neighbors. To this day, I'm extremely careful when walking into any street, and I watch over my kids, as well. My mother did protect me that day. She spoke to the parent of the young girl who got hit, and things got better.

As you can imagine, this event traumatized me. Time went on, but I sought an escape. Chaz consoled me about the car incident, and that made me feel much better.

We continued our talks, and I started to ask him about sex. I was feeling the urge to explore my sexual desires again, and I could feel my demons come to life. Our house was almost empty, there were no movies to watch, no older women coming to parties, and I was going through withdrawal.

"Chaz, can I tell you something?"

"Sure, go ahead." Chaz knew how I was feeling. He just knew me well.

"I've been thinking about sex a lot lately, like a whole lot. Is that normal?"

"Yes, that's quite normal. Your hormones are changing, Doubleo. That's fine."

"But it's pretty intense. Like I get a feeling of wanting a girl very bad, you know?"

"Yes, I do know, and that's natural."

"But there's something else."

"Something else? Like what?"

"I was touched by Marco, a family member, and I was also molested by my babysitter," I told him in a low voice, embarrassed.

"Oh damn. Are you serious? When did this happen?"

"Yes, I'm very serious. Please don't tell anyone, okay? It happened some time ago, but no one in my family knows. I think I'm okay, but I don't really know. I think about those things all the time."

"Darn, Doubleo, come here. You need a hug."

"Yeah, I do. I really do. Wait, don't hug me too long."

We laughed.

"You know you're like a lady."

We laughed again, and he hugged me and told me it was going to be okay. "Sit down. We need to talk for a moment. See, things have happened to me, to you, and to lots of people. Things have happened to your mother, too."

"Yeah, it's just a lot. I don't have no kind of escape, and it's gettin' painful. I think about all of those things, but my feelings are what I want to talk about."

"What kind of feelings?"

"They're sexual. I feel like something is trapped inside me. It's like an exciting feeling, like when I was molested. That felt good. I know this sounds weird."

Chaz cut me off. "No it doesn't. It doesn't sound weird at all. I understand."

"Okay, so how do I get rid of this sexual feeling, like a feeling that I need to come out of my body, or something like that?"

"Come out of your body? What do you mean?"

"Like, I've been thinking about my babysitter a lot, what she did to me, and how it felt. I actually want that feeling again."

"You do?"

"Yeah, very bad."

"Okay, well there are a few things you can do. You can . . ."

I cut Chaz off. "My penis gets hard."

"That's nature," he responded.

"Okay, I don't want to know about nature. I want to be like, outside of myself, like, I want that rape, molestation feeling again. Even though what she did was bad, the feeling wasn't bad at all."

"Oh, I see. Well, let me ask you a question."

"Sure, go ahead."

"Have you ever heard of masturbation?"

"No, what's that?" I asked hesitantly.

"Men and women do it. They touch themselves on their private area for pleasure."

"They do? You can make yourself feel good by doing that?"

"Yes, yes, you can, but I'm not going to go into further detail. I will say this. You'll feel better, and you might come outside of your body. It's okay to touch yourself. It's really okay."

"Yeah, I guess so. Other people have touched me."

We laughed.

"Good thing you have a sense of humor about it."

"Yeah, I really do. Okay, I'm gonna go touch myself."

"Okay," he said. "Be gentle. I hate to say this, but since you liked the person who molested you, think about her, and when you get excited, you'll feel better."

"I still think about her. I really do."

Chaz told me about masturbation, I had never masturbated in my life, but I now knew how, and I was twelve years old. It helped. I was outside of my body, and I loved it.

CHAPTER 20

Eviction—Homeless

After graduating from the 6th grade,
this is what I came home to

**FINAL
EVICTION
NOTIFICATION**

Cleveland Municipal Court
Housing Division
BAILIFF'S DEPARTMENT
JUSTICE CENTER — COURTS TOWER
1200 ONTARIO STREET
THIRD FLOOR

Defendant _____

Address _____

Date _____ Case No. _____

ATTENTION

The Court has ordered you to vacate and leave
the premises you now occupy.
　　Unless this order is complied with, your
property and effects will be moved into the street
without further notice to you or placed in storage.

BE OUT BEFORE

I didn't want to leave our house,
I thought peeling this off would help, it didn't

WE LOST OUR house the day I graduated from sixth grade. Waking up that morning, getting ready for my graduation, I surely didn't expect to come home and see what I saw. I'm not sure if my brother or sister knew, but when I walked home from Chambers Elementary School that day, I quickly found out.

Graduation was over and I headed home, about a twenty-minute walk. The majority of the path from school to my house was through a park and past the school and pool that we played and swam in. Graduation went well, and I was ready for the seventh grade. All I could think about was a somewhat better life ahead of me, but that wasn't to be the case. Passing the old baseball field that we played on as kids, the stadium that Shaw High School football played in, and the pool that we had so much fun in would become an old memory. With the exception of the football field, neither my siblings nor I would ever use them again, though I didn't know this at the time.

Meanwhile, as I got closer to our home, I could see what looked like trash in front of our house. As I came nearer, I realized that it wasn't trash. It was our furniture. We were being evicted, and I was sure we had nowhere to go. I would later learn that there had been a plan in place, but at the time, I had no idea.

As I approached the house, I saw my brother bringing items from inside and setting them on the lawn: my clothes, some toys, and more of our furniture. I also saw a big red piece of paper on the front door that said, *EVICTION NOTICE.* That scared the hell out of me, but there wasn't anything that I could do.

"Mommy lost the house," my brother said, "and we have to move."

I asked him where we were moving to.

"Well, I don't know about you and Toni," he said, "but me and Mommy are moving to the Townhouse Motel on Euclid. Oh, and the lights are out, the phone is off, and there isn't any water."

I fell to the ground on the front lawn in my graduation clothes, crying my eyes out, with nowhere to go, and now homeless. "Why does this keep happening to our family?" I screamed out. "Why?"

I just wanted to know why our life was so painful and shook up. I was still trying hard to figure out why my parents divorced, and why we were being evicted. I had no answers, so I tried to put things together. Not long before we were evicted, I found out that I had another brother I hadn't known about, the one I finally met in 1979. Maybe this was part of the reason for my parents' divorce, but I never found out the entire reason why.

Our house was mostly empty. Only a few items lay around. We were all outside—my brother, sister, and me—just looking at our belongings on the lawn. They headed inside for a little while, and I stayed outside staring at the pile of furniture, beds, trash, old clothes. It was embarrassing.

I met my other brother, Ralph, in 1979. He was nineteen and living in Butler, Alabama. We hadn't known that. I remember the day my father told my mother. We were at home, and they were drinking when he told her. I heard them downstairs talking and arguing. I went downstairs and found my father crying.

"Daddy, what's wrong?" I asked.

He fought to speak through his tears. "Man, don't be mad, but, but . . . you have another brother."

"Where is he?" I asked.

"He's in Alabama, and your mother won't accept him."

What was I to say? I didn't know if my father had cheated, or if my mother just didn't know he had a son before they met. Either way, I couldn't wait to meet him.

Eviction day was hot and heavy. I stared at the big red sign on our front door. I wanted so bad to tear it down. It was huge, with bold, black letters. Everyone could see it.

In the almost empty house, Chaz and my mother continued to smoke plenty of weed, regardless of our situation. I guess the weed helped them deal with the eviction because Chaz had to find somewhere else to live, too. Every time we came home, you could smell the weed all through the house. It smelled great to me, but what did I know? My parents and their friends always smoked weed at their parties, and that was probably why I was so horny when they had them. Chaz and my mother would smoke weed all night and just talk about everything: politics, God, sex, you name it. They were high and deep in their conversations, and so was I. Contact highs were plentiful, and that's probably why I always felt like I was a weird kid.

It was starting to get dark. I wandered around the house. There was no food, no water, and now it was dusk. Our household goods were still on the lawn, and I was a total mess. Previously, I would always go to the front door to see if my father would drive down the street in that ugly blue car, but those days were over. The divorce was final. The house was so empty, you could hear echoes.

On this night, I was bored. I went to the front screen door just to look out and see the darkness. There wasn't anything else to do really. I could hear my next-door neighbor's parents arguing and fighting. I could even hear glass break. As kids, between my household and the neighbors', we would always hear each other's parents fighting.

I looked down the street, just to see if my father was coming, but I knew he wasn't. I did this often, hoping that he would appear.

Then, all of a sudden, I saw a car that seemed to be his. *Is this my father?* I thought. *Is this my father?* I could hear his old-school music slowly floating from the car windows. It had to be him, I told myself. The car moved at a snail's pace as the sun slowly set. I heard the O'Jays, a song he played often: "Cry Together." It seemed like when he played that song, he was trying to say something to my mother.

The car pulled up in front of our house. "Doubleo," the man yelled, "come here, man. I have a surprise for you."

"Hey, Daddy, what's up?" I ran to the car.

"Get in. We're going to pick your brother up from the bus station."

"For real?" I said, smiling as if he just gave me a bunch of candy.

"Hop in."

"Okay, Daddy, let's go."

We headed to downtown Cleveland, the Greyhound station.

"Get out," my dad said. "Let's go get your brother."

"Cool," I responded. "Daddy, what's his name?"

"His name is Ralph."

"Okay, cool. I can't wait."

"Yeah, me either," my dad said. "I haven't seen him in a long time. I hope I remember how he looks."

"I bet he's dark just like you."

We laughed hard, holding our stomachs and bending over.

"You nervous?" my dad asked.

"Yeah, I am, just a little, but I'm more happy about seeing him."

"Cool," my father replied. "I am, too, man."

We arrived at the terminal. My hands were sweating, my heart beat fast, and I was nervous as hell. "Daddy, are you nervous?"

"Yeah, man, I am. I am for real."

"Hey, Dad," someone yelled.

The voice sounded like my father's voice. I knew it had to be my brother. My dad and I turned around at the same time.

"Hey, man, what's going on, Ralph?"

My brother put down his luggage, and they hugged.

"Happy to be here, Dad. That bus ride from Alabama was long."

"This is your little brother, Doubleo," my father said.

I looked up at Ralph. He was six feet tall, maybe a little taller, and he weighed about 180 or 190 pounds, all muscle, just like a country boy. He was dark just like our father, with a miniature Afro and thick sideburns. He wore jeans and a blue shirt with cutoff sleeves.

I couldn't believe I was seeing my brother. I stood there in shock for a few minutes, then broke my silence. "Hey, Ralph," I said, "nice to meet you."

We shook hands, and then he said, "Man, give me a hug. I'm yo brotha!"

Those words shook me to my core. My brother that I never knew or saw before hugged me tight. I didn't want to let go. All of my emotions ran through me, all of the thoughts of being groped, molested, the divorce, being evicted, just came out of me. It was like my brother was a savior to me that day.

We grabbed his suitcase and left the bus station.

"Y'all hungry?" my father asked.

"Yeah, Daddy. Let's get some burgers."

"Ralph, what you want?" my father asked.

"I'm cool with what Doubleo wants," he said as he looked back at me in the backseat.

I smiled. "Yea, McDonald's!" I shouted. "Yea, burgers!"

We all laughed.

It was dark out now. "Okay, Dub, we're going to take you home now. I know your mother is looking for you."

"Okay, Daddy, that's cool," I responded, even though I didn't want to go back to that empty house. There wasn't any water or electricity. It was horrible.

* * *

Days went by. We were still gathering a few things from the house. We were almost done cleaning up and ready to move. As I looked out the door, I saw a huge green truck coming down the street. It was loud and heavy. As the truck got closer, it slowed down. It was pitch-black outside, and my fears were beginning to come back.

"Who is this?" I said to myself. "I have no clue."

The truck pulled into our yard, the person quietly came into the driveway, and then stopped. I could barely see the person get out of the truck. I was hoping that it was my father. Maybe my parents were getting back together. I had no clue, but then I heard another of my father's favorite songs, one by Isaac Hayes called "I Stand Accused." I could barely see a man, but the music was slow, old-school, just like the music my father listened to.

He was smoking a cigarette as he got out of his truck. I smelled the smoke, and I could see the flame from his cigarette, but I heard no voice. From the looks of it, he walked just like my father. His movements were just like my father's movements. I felt like I knew this person, but I wasn't sure.

Then he stopped, jumped in the back of the truck, sat there, and turned up a bottle of liquor. He usually drank 151 gin, with a chaser, a small cup of water. I'd seen my father do this over and over again when we were at the juke joints on Seventieth and Hough. This night, he turned a bottle up, but no water, and no cup for small sips.

His drinking had increased, and his eyes were tired. He looked worn-down, not from work, but from losing his family. After his gulp of the 151 gin, straight, he put the bottle on the lift gate and whispered, "Hey, Doubleo, it's me, your father."

I immediately started crying. I wanted my father back in the house, but I knew that if my mother heard us talking, she would call the police. The house was so empty, an echo would carry far, and right up to my mother's room. Regardless, I wanted my parents back together. I had no clue what had caused the divorce. Was it my father's infidelity? Was it my mother's infidelity? I knew something had happened.

Duke, our dog, was howling in the backyard, as if he knew about all the drama.

Then my father said, "I have to take the dog and the TV."

We only had one TV in the house by this time, and it was a nineteen-inch set with broken antennas and a hanger sticking up out of the back for reception.

I begged him to let us keep the TV and the dog, but he said we couldn't have the dog because my sister and I might be going to a foster home. I fell to the floor again, flooded with tears and pain over losing my father and being homeless, hungry, and dirty. My father asked me to help him put Duke in the truck so he could leave, and I cried again. We put the dog in the truck, and then my father lit another cigarette.

This time he paused, took a drag of his cigarette, looked at me, and said, "I'm going to burn this fucking house down."

For some reason, I looked back as if already seeing the house burning. I quickly turned back to my father and started crying.

"Daddy, please don't," I whispered. "Don't burn it down. Don't hurt us."

My mother, brother, sister, and Mr. Chaz were in the house. Could I save them if my father did try to burn the house down? Maybe not. Saving them was my second thought. My first was to leave at that moment with my father.

He stood up—tall, dark, and mean-looking with his Ford Motor Company coveralls on—as if he was ready to start the fire. He was looking up at my mother's bedroom window in front of the house as if he was reminiscing about their times together. His eyes were red, his mouth was tight, so I just knew it was over. I knew that my family was about to perish in a ball of fire.

"Go back in the house," he said. "I'm not going to burn it down." Off my father went.

This was the end for me. I hated life and everything that it stood for. That lonely night in the driveway with my father was another turning point in my life, a turning point for the worse. I loved my father dearly, and I wanted to impress him. He had actually given me an idea, and he didn't know it.

CHAPTER 21

The Twelve-Year-Old Arsonist

I WAS SURELY MY father's child. He left an indelible mark on me with his demeanor, the way he walked, talked, laughed, and interacted with people. He definitely made me think about burning the house down. After all that I had gone through—being molested, fondled, bullied, losing a home and being homeless, and a host of other things—you would think that I had been through enough. And not one time was there any help for me, no intervention. Most times, I didn't care about right from wrong. I did know better, but most bad things simply motivated me, gave me a sense of excitement, and in some twisted way, gave me a sense of accomplishment. What would get worse in a normal kid's mind got better in mine. Angry, and full of rage, not knowing where we were going to live, I felt like if we couldn't have that house, then no one could.

I attempted to burn the house down after my father left. I tried on two occasions. The first time that I did it, I happened to be in the kitchen while my mother was on the phone. All

I wanted were two things: her attention and a grilled ham and cheese sandwich.

While my mother was on the phone, I paced back and forth. I had nothing else to do. My stomach was empty, and I felt ignored, pissed off, irritated. Both my mother and father smoked, so there was always a lighter and matches in the kitchen drawer. The feeling of my mother ignoring me poured over me with intensity. I could hear her on the phone with her friend, laughing and having a good time. Maybe I didn't get her attention, or maybe I did. I didn't feel as though I did. I just felt ignored. That feeling, coupled with being hungry, drew pure anger from deep down in my soul, and I had to do something. I needed to act out. It was like I needed a release.

I felt a sense of anticipation growing inside of me as the anger boiled over and I paced in the kitchen. I looked over and saw a book of matches in the drawer. I noticed a pile of napkins on the other side of the counter. In my mind, that was the perfect combination to start a fire. I grabbed a napkin, struck a match, held it to the napkin, and the small blaze started.

On the other side of the kitchen was the garbage can. It was beneath the cabinet and below the phone, so when the blaze started to rise, the phone cord would be the second thing to burn. Since my mother was on the phone, the cord was stretched into the other room where she was. After I set the napkin on fire, I threw it in the garbage can, and immediately the fire shot up the wall. Without saying anything, I ran outside and up the street.

The fire burned the phone cord, which disconnected the call and brought my mother to the other end of the cord. At that point, she saw the garbage can, the wall, and the phone cord on fire. Smoke filled the kitchen. My mother yelled for all of us to come help, but I was nowhere to be found. My brother put the fire out, and they came to look for me. He found me halfway down the street and brought me home, where I got my ass beat.

The second time I tried to burn the house down, I was in the basement. My father was an avid reader of the *Plain Dealer*, our local newspaper. He never threw the papers away once he was done reading, so they were piled high in the basement and stayed there for years. For years, while my father lived with us, my mother never read the newspaper, and she told me why. She stated that it literally drove her crazy to keep picking the papers up after my father read them. He'd leave papers all over the house, so she just gave up reading the newspaper. As it turned out, the papers did serve a purpose. During the time that my parents were married, my mother had become a den mother for my Cub Scout troop, Pack 331. She collected the papers and then turned them in for recycling to make money for my Cub Scout pack.

The day I did what I did, we wouldn't get much money, if any, for the newspapers in the basement. Still angry and hurt from the divorce, I went downstairs, looked around, and saw the huge pile of papers. I ran back upstairs, got a book of matches, struck a match, and threw it into the pile of papers. The blaze caught on quickly, and I ran out of the house again.

My brother came to the rescue this time, too. They all came and got me, and I got my ass beat again. I failed twice at trying to burn the house down, and that was a good thing. That was the last time I tried.

CHAPTER 22

The Stare That Saved My Life

Time to end it all

Damaged people are dangerous.
They know how to make hell feel like home.

I'VE HAD ENOUGH of this shit, I thought. *I'm tired of being dirty, hungry, poor, and helpless. I'm done.*

Being mentally strong like my mother, I could deal with a lot of shit. I had no idea, back then, that I could process the most painful encounters, setbacks, failures, and letdowns, and still remain sane. I wanted to jump out the bathroom window and just get it over with. If I remember correctly, our bathroom window was about twenty-five feet or so from the ground. The distance from our house and the neighbors' house was probably fifteen feet. It was rather close, so privacy wasn't there.

At eleven years old, I knew that my chances of dying from the jump would be pretty good. My mind made up, I went upstairs in the now empty house, entered the bathroom, and opened the window. I sat there, peeking out the window, my head barely up above the lower windowsill, ready to end it all. Directly across the way, I saw Mrs. Shell looking out her window at me.

I respected all of my elders, especially my next-door neighbors. Mrs. Shell and her husband had by far the most musically talented kids in East Cleveland. They played every instrument known to man. One of her sons played with or practiced with one of the Marsalis brothers—I'm not sure if it was Wynton or Branford. Either way, they were musically inclined, all five of them.

I looked out to the front porch of our neighbors' house and saw that Mrs. Shell was now sitting there, facing the street. I could see her back. She was wearing a pair of cutoff blue jeans and a cotton shirt with no sleeves, drinking her soda and reading the newspaper. Most days when Mrs. Shell was on the porch, she'd watch the kids zooming up and down the street, telling them to slow down—cars, too. If you were speeding, by the time you got close to Mrs. Shell's house, you had better slow down. She didn't play.

I was ready to jump. I couldn't take it anymore. This life had become too much to handle. I looked in the bathroom mirror, checking myself out, and all I saw was an empty little kid, withdrawn. I knew then that I had nothing left—no feelings, no tears. I was all out of everything.

I turned to my right, faced the window, and walked three paces. As I looked out to make sure the coast was clear, I hung my left leg out the window. All I had to do next was to get the other one out and jump. Once my leg was out, I peeked out to make sure no one was there.

As I opened the upstairs window higher, high enough to squeeze out, it made a squeaking noise. The wood window pane was rubbing against the frame of the window, and now my cover was blown.

What I saw was Mrs. Shell staring up at me, motionless. She

uttered her famous words, words that in the past had stopped any and all kids right in their tracks. "You had better not. Now get your ass back in that window."

I did so, hesitantly, and as I got back inside, I sat on the floor and cried my eyes out. My brothers and sister never knew about this, nor did my parents.

Mrs. Shell took great care of us. She fed us and gave us juice, popsicles, sandwiches, and candy, and for that, I always had great respect for her and her husband. She didn't take shit from anyone in the neighborhood.

Those words were all I needed to hear. She knew we were going through hard times and could tell that I was on the verge of ending it all. I was done. I was ready to kill myself. At that moment, all I needed to know was that someone cared, someone knew what we were going through, and that times would get better. I couldn't see that far out. My mind and judgment were clouded, and I had but one answer. I was unsuccessful once again. The stare of Mrs. Shell saved my life.

CHAPTER 23

The Long and Winding Road

After we lost the house,
this is where my mother and brother lived

I hated this place, so I stole from and
broke their candy machines

LEAVING OUR HOME on Alder Avenue in East Cleveland was extremely painful. Our belongings had sat on the lawn for a few days. We'd lived in darkness for some time, we lacked food, and cold water was all we had unless we warmed it up. We had no light other than the sun. For some reason, our mother seemed okay with living like this, but I wasn't.

"Get your shit, man, we have to go," my brother said.

"Huh? Where are we going?"

"Well, me and Mommy are moving to the Townhouse Motel on Euclid, like I told you before. Toni is going to Eileen's daughter's house, and I guess you're going to Eileen's house."

"Does Eileen know that I am coming?"

"I don't know. Ask Mommy."

"Ma, does she know I'm coming?"

"Yes, Doubleo, she knows. You'll stay there for a little while, but don't worry. We'll all be back together one day."

I never thought that I would just walk down the street and my family would head in separate directions. It was devastating to think about, but it was worse to actually see it all play out. We put all our stuff, which wasn't much, in little buggies, the ones with two wheels and a basket. I didn't even have time to say goodbye to my neighbors.

We started our walk down the street in the rain and cold, passing all my friends' houses. I had no gloves and wore a small jacket that was torn to shit. We were soaking wet. It seemed like a death march, like the ones that Jewish families and American soldiers had to take many years ago. The only difference was that we weren't being shot or drowned. My soul was slowly being killed: it was painful, it was cold, and I was being separated from my family. It sucked. What was especially horrible about it was that I could see up ahead the corner where we would go our separate ways: Coit and Taylor. That would be the execution point where our cohesiveness would be taken away.

I felt like a piece of trash, just like the toys and trash on our front lawn. There wasn't any difference in my mind. My anger grew. I was already empty and emotionless, but this took me over the top for sure. That was it. It was that easy. We were a broken family.

My mother and brother were walking together, my sister and me as well, and we were all headed in the same direction at that moment. We were a complete family for the last time for about forty-five minutes until I peeled off to another street and headed to Eileen's house. That day was the last time we were together as a family until a year later. To be away from your family, not living together for a year, is a long time. That one year changed me tremendously, forever.

As we all walked down Alder Avenue, for some reason that day, all of my friends were outside at the other end of the street playing in the rain. They could see that we were packed up, walking, and homeless. When I saw each friend, I said goodbye, hugged them, and cried. My mother and brother went one way, my sister went another way, and I went another. We were all split up and headed to three different places to live. I walked about two to three miles to Eileen's house, the longest walk in my life.

To this day, when I lose something that's not family, I couldn't care less. Either I find a way to get it again, or I just take a loss and don't give a shit about it. It's not a good way to be, because most people take it as if I don't care. The truth is that I've been so tired and hurt from loss that I'm afraid to feel that pain again, so I discount the loss as unimportant to me, and I block out my love for anything.

I finished my walk and got to Eileen's house. She knew that I was coming over. Man, all I wanted was a nice, hot, grilled cheese sandwich, some chips, and then some grape Kool-Aid to wash it down. That's it: something simple. I craved small things. I just wanted to know that someone cared, that was all.

I arrived at Eileen's house and rang the doorbell.

Her son answered. "Hey," he said. "I'm Larry. How are you?"

"I'm good, man. I'm Doubleo. how are you?"

We shook hands, and he invited me in. There was a couch to the right, white, covered with plastic. An old TV sat on a frail gold frame, with three glasses on each shelf. Thick curtains adorned the windows, and the floors had carpet all the way through the house. In the other room, there was more furniture: two more couches, and another TV, much larger than the other one. The house smelled like well-seasoned pot roast, potatoes, and corn bread. Then I smelled greens simmering, just like my grandmother cooked, and I could smell a cake in the oven also. I knew that smell all too well. On the stereo, I could hear "Ain't Too Proud to Beg," by the Temptations. Harsh reminders, but this scene was much different.

I felt at home as soon as I walked in their house and saw Eileen walk confidently down the stairs. "Hey, Doubleo, about time you got here, boy," she said, as she hugged me with all of her might.

Short in stature, with dark brown skin and a thick, glossy Afro, she stood five feet three. She wore round earrings and a dab of ruby red lipstick, not too thick. Flip-flops covered her feet, and she was wearing a short-sleeved black shirt with blue jeans. She smelled good, too.

"Yeah, I know, Mrs. Eileen. It was hard leaving our house and leaving my family."

"I know, sweetie," she said, giving me another hug.

I cried just a little. Her hug felt good, and I felt refreshed.

"Are you hungry?"

"Yes, please, I'm starving."

"Okay, gimme those wet clothes. Larry, go get him some clean dry ones from the basement." I had only brought a few items from the house we had lost, and I needed new clothes bad.

"Mrs. Eileen?"

"Yes, Doubleo?" she responded.

"That food smells really good. I love that smell."

"Okay, you know we eat good over here. You're more than welcome to eat whatever you want."

Besides the other food, she had made me some warm chicken noodle soup, and I smiled like a little baby drinking some warm milk. My belly hadn't been filled like that in such a long time. Now that was a great feeling.

Larry brought some clean clothes and took me upstairs. He showed me my room, the bed, where the towels were, and then gave me a complete tour of the house.

I felt really good about staying there. They had lights, heat, air conditioning, a nice TV, food. It was like heaven to me. After all, I hadn't slept in a bed in a couple of years. I had been on the floor because of my bed-wetting.

Eileen and Larry helped me get back on my feet. As I settled in, they fed me and bought clothes for me from Goodwill. I was now in the seventh grade. It had probably been a few months since I had seen my mother, brother, and sister, though we were only about a half mile away from each other. I craved having my family back together. I still had a little hope that we could reunite, and I had to find out if it was possible.

One day when I got back to Eileen's house after school, I decided to go see my mother and brother. I had no idea what they would say to me, but I had to go. I just wanted to see their faces.

My heart beat fast. I was nervous. What would I say to my mother? After all, I still felt like she just threw me away. I was basically on my own, though Eileen and her son made me feel comfortable.

I jogged down the street to the Townhouse Motel, about a block away. The lady at the front desk asked me what I wanted.

"I'm looking for my mother."

"Well, then you need to check in, because I don't recognize you."

I explained who my mother was, and she gave me the room number. I ran back down the hall and knocked on the door. When my mother opened the door, I hugged her tightly. I missed her so much. I was shaking in her arms.

We chatted a little, and then the conversation changed. "You look just like your father. You smell like him, you walk like him, and you sound like him."

All the while, she had a disgusted look on her face, as if she wasn't even happy to see me. I was crushed again. I walked around the motel room in hopes of seeing an extra room for my sister and me. "Mommy, when are we moving back in together?"

"Doubleo, kids can't live here. I don't know when we'll be back together."

I wasn't expecting to hear that at all. My feelings were crushed. I then asked her for money to get a snack from the snack machine out in the lobby.

"I'm broke," she said. "I don't have any money."

I went out to the lobby, and the man for the snack machine was changing the snacks out and refilling the machine. I noticed that he dropped a quarter but just let it roll under the machine. Once he was done, I looked for the quarter and found it, plus an additional two to three dollars' worth of coins under the machine. I ate a bunch of junk that day: Snickers, Now and Laters, PayDays, Hershey bars, Honey Buns.

Later, after getting more coins from another bar, I walked

down to Sisters' Chicken and Biscuits on Euclid Avenue in East Cleveland, then back up the street to Jack's doughnuts.

For the next year or so, when going to see my mother, I figured, *Hell, she won't have any money*, so before I went in to see her, or even ask for money, I'd look under that machine, telling the lady that I had dropped a quarter and borrowing her yardstick. I'd sweep it under the machine, where there was always a bunch of change. I'd swipe under those machines for twenty to thirty minutes, long enough to get all of those coins. This became my routine—not just at the Townhouse Motel, but in any building, store, or hotel that had snack and pop machines, all up and down Euclid Avenue.

I lived with Eileen and her son for maybe a year. Her son was a great kid. We got along extremely well, and he took me in just like his mother did. To this day, I owe him a lot. We were like brothers, but I was so lost, I had no clue how to thank them, or my little buddy. I ate well at their house, made new friends in that neighborhood, and life was getting better—much better. Our family was still broken, but sometimes it even felt like it didn't matter. I felt like my mother had given up on us and given us away, and I believe now that this was the start of me not wanting to ever love another woman again.

CHAPTER 24

Floor Boy

It was dirty, and I itched throughout my 8th grade year

My new bed, again

A YEAR HAD GONE by when I came home from school one mild day in 1980 to hear Eileen say, "Doubleo, I have some good news."

"Oh yeah?" I replied. "What's that. Mrs. Eileen?"

"Your mother found a home for you and your sister, and you can all go over there today if you're ready."

I cried my eyes out when she told me this. I had grown used to life with her and life without my mother. I was comfortable at Eileen's house. I had made some friends, and we were eating good every day. Moreover, she had a washing machine, a dryer, heat, and air conditioning. It was nice, and I didn't want to leave that. Furthermore, I had no clue where we would live with my mother. Actually, I didn't trust the new place, but I had to go. I packed my clothes and hugged Larry and Eileen.

Eileen gave me the address and asked if I had money to catch the bus.

I had money that I had scraped from under the candy machines at the hotels, bars, and stores. I gave her a quick thumbs-up. "I'm good."

She looked at me and smiled.

I smiled back.

"Boy, you're something else. You're going to be all right."

We hugged tightly. I cried. She cried. I didn't want to go. Her house felt like home for me, something I hadn't felt for years. Then I left. I caught the bus down Euclid to the Rapid station. As I got off the bus, I walked up the street—Knowles, off Euclid. Our new place was right down the street from Kirk Junior High School, so I thought that was pretty cool.

I got to the house and rang the doorbell.

A big, dark, ugly-ass man answered the door. "Who are you?" he said.

"I'm Doubleo, Sylvia's son."

"I didn't know she had another son," he replied.

I was pissed again, but this time, I didn't cry.

He told me to hold on, then yelled upstairs, "Hey, Sylvia, some little boy is down here."

I heard my mother yell from upstairs, "Let him in. That's my son."

I headed upstairs, dragging my bag of clothes with me. I made it to the top and entered the apartment. I looked around and entered the first room. It was small, maybe about ten feet by ten feet max, with a low, dusty ceiling full of spider webs and an old, dirty carpet that smelled of cat urine. It had a small bed, a dresser shoved in the corner, and a small lamp with a dim light. It wasn't what I was expecting.

I looked in the kitchen and noticed that it was small as hell. The table was the size of a small patio table, brown in color, with chipped and cracked corners. The salt and pepper shakers that stood on top were empty. I immediately felt hungry. It seemed like I was back where we were when we got evicted, bare-bones all over again.

I checked the bathroom. It had a small tub, an even smaller sink, and no shower curtain. The window had a crack going straight through the center. It seemed to be made of thick plexiglass, frosted. I couldn't see out of it. I felt trapped as if in a jail cell, only smaller. The floor was peeling, and a few tiles were missing. You could see the old wooden floor in places.

Next I went to my mother's bedroom, which was just as small as the bathroom. She had a twin bed, one window, a tray table with an ashtray full of cigarette butts, an old brown dresser, and a broken mirror that stood about five feet and leaned up against the wall. That was it. That was where we were living, all four of us. I couldn't believe it, but that was all that my mother could afford.

I saw my brother and sister, and I hugged them. My brother was sitting on the bed, and my sister was sitting on the floor, so I sat on the floor, too. It was nice to finally be back together again. We talked, laughed, and just stared at each other. I missed them dearly, and it was like we didn't even know each other. A year had passed, we had all grown some, and they both looked different to me, but we had a chance to start all over again.

Overall, the place at 1833 Knowles in East Cleveland was small as hell. In all, it had a bathroom, a kitchen, one bedroom, and a makeshift room, no bigger than a jail cell, that the three of us made our little home for the remainder of the year. It really sucked.

My happiness at being together quickly drew to a close. Things were rough. We barely had food to eat, and I didn't have any decent clothes. The pants I wore didn't have a zipper. They were tight, and my shoes were all run over. My pants were brown, with yellow stripes going down the sides, high on the ankles, but it didn't matter. That was all I had. I wore those pants for a long time, and the shoes, too. The carpet was nasty. It was that old-ass spotted leopard carpet, with a half inch of matting under it. That didn't help or make it better.

My mother took another bar job around the corner from our house, but it didn't really help. It sucked, too, because everyone knew that my mother was a barmaid again. One thing for sure, the bar had some great food. After school, my mother would have the chef make me a very good burger. Not having food much of the time, I developed an appreciation for food that I still have to this day.

My mother had finally found a boyfriend, a guy she met at the bar, the guy who opened the door when I first came to the house. I hated his ass, too. He was ugly and smoked cigarettes and had bad breath and ugly teeth. He wore dreadful clothes and thick glasses. My mother really stooped low for this guy, a far cry from my father. I wasn't rude to him, but I never talked to his ass—never. We were used to seeing a tall, dark, strong man with a serious presence in the house. This dude was the total opposite, and we didn't like him.

When I graduated from the eighth grade in 1980, there was a ceremony at Kirk Junior High for those who were leaving and headed to Shaw High School. Kirk was a good school, but it had some serious bullies. They all looked much older than we did, like they should have been in the tenth grade. The school was great for us and turned out some great athletes, too.

The ceremony commenced, but as I looked out into the crowd, I didn't see my mother. How could she not be there? The school was right up the street from our house and the bar. When I went home after everything was over, I decided to stop in the bar to see if I could find my mother. There she was, serving drinks to these old, dirty-ass men. I was pissed.

At that moment, I made up my mind to move in with my father. My sister decided to as well, but it wouldn't be that easy. If it happened, we knew that life would be a little better. At least we would be able to get clothes and some food. I could say goodbye to that old-ass, spotted leopard carpet with the matting that was my bed for my entire eighth grade year. Back to the floor I'd go. That was home for me. I knew it all too well.

The best way out is always through.

—*Robert Frost*

CHAPTER 25

Ku Klux Klan in a Suit

This place made me hate judges and lawyers

Which foster home will we be heading to

Set your goals for someone else.
If you let yourself down, no one will know.
If you let someone else down, now you have a witness.
—*Leon R. Walker Jr.*

I NEVER KNEW WHAT it was like for my ancestors to be slaves. I had no clue. I didn't know what it was like to have them separated from their siblings—or immediate family, for that matter—by the mean, racist slave masters. I had no clue what that felt like.

However, I watched the movie *Roots* when I was in the sixth grade, a sad movie that made me feel something. I distinctly remember how the slave owners took over and dominated the black families and broke them apart. They whipped and tortured the dominant male in the house, slapped the wife or mother, and bullied and yelled at the kids while they entered and took over the house.

Even though shown in a movie, the story was tragic and shook me to my core. Those thoughts and memories have never left my soul and never will. Divorce lawyers, social workers, and family psychiatrists seem to have the same effect on me. Even though, nowadays, at least in the northern part of the country, blacks aren't hung or whipped, the separating of families is and has always been assisted by those professionals that I just mentioned.

I hate lawyers, even to this day. I hated my ex-wife's lawyer, too. He didn't do anything to me, but he was chunky and aggressive. I didn't like big black lawyers, either. They were intimidating, loud, scary, and disrespectful. They defended people who should have gone to the electric chair, and even broke up families like those men in *Roots*. I hated them all.

* * *

As soon as I got home from school one day, I heard my mother say, "Doubleo, you and Toni have court today." She showed me a letter from the courthouse instructing us to appear in court to determine if my sister and I were going to a foster home because the apartment we were living in was too small and unfit for a family of four.

I got sick as I read the letter, terrified. Was I going to be snatched from my family and put with a group of people that I didn't know? White families back then would take in a black child in an instant, and they still do to this day. Sometimes, I felt like I would be better off with a white family. They had nice vehicles, lots of food, big houses, nice clean animals, a house full of laughter, toys, minibikes, go-karts. They had it all. I was confused and worried. How would I make it with another family?

My sister and I talked about the court visit. We had no clue what to expect. I was fourteen and she was thirteen. I remember the day we went. It was on a weekday. My father called to tell me what time he was coming to pick us up.

Even though my father had a good job at Ford, the divorce left him with child support to pay for three kids, so his living conditions weren't really that good. I, too, had this situation later in life. Had I thought about my fathers situation, I could have come out better in my own marriage. I would have taken heed to what marriage is all about. I would have managed the household better, been a better father, and a better husband. I didn't take heed to hindsight, nor did I value my wedding vowels. I'm not saying that my father didn't do these things, or that he wasn't a great husband or father. He was. But as a young kid, being so young when my parents divorced, and because of my inability to process great parenting, divorce, and the impacts of it all, I was doomed to repeat those actions.

I remember anxiously looking out the window of my mother's apartment on the day of court. I saw my father pull up, and my eyes lit up at the sight of him. He was driving a burgundy Monte Carlo. I smiled and waved out the window.

He whistled. "Let's go, boy. We need to be downtown by ten."

"Toni, Daddy's here. Let's go."

It was as if we were already moving out of that little-ass house and my days of sleeping on the floor were over, though not the case quite just yet. I couldn't wait for court to be over, but I knew that it wasn't going to be that easy.

My sister and I got dressed, and off we went. We got on the freeway and headed downtown, taking I-90 West, then got off on Ninth Street. I remember looking up at the tall buildings. It was cold out, and I could see the Cleveland Browns stadium after we made our exit from the freeway, more tall buildings, and then the damn courthouse.

As we exited my father's car, we entered the building and then headed to one of the cold, strong, stone-encased rooms. As we entered, I noticed a huge brown desk. Wide and made of solid oak, it seemed ten feet tall.

Rising up from behind that huge desk was a big white chunky man. I remember his stubby fingers rolling around on his desk, as if he was ready to ship my sister and me off to another family. "Walker family," he shouted, "please come up."

He was dressed in a nice suit, far from what my father had on. Dad was wearing his Ford Motor Company coveralls that day. All I can remember is that the judge wore a button-down shirt, and the fat from his thick neck hung down over his collar, which was a bit dirty. He was sweating profusely.

This man has had a long day, I thought.

And boy, was he mean. He had a big head, a fat nose, greasy hair, and thick bifocal glasses. I remember him to this day.

As we stepped closer, my sister and I held hands, kind of like what you see little kids do when they don't know any better.

We stepped up inch by inch, and as we slowly got closer to this man, he seemed to get bigger and bigger. It was a frightening scene. I hated him already, and he hadn't even said a word. As we crept closer, I looked at my sister and she looked at me. We were both in tears and looking like we were about to be slaughtered. I could feel my sister's hands start to sweat. There we were, two little poor kids, their father, and more issues for him to deal with.

As we approached the desk, the judge shook my father's hand and looked at us as if he were saying, "Well, well, more little nigger kids from a broken family." Had he said that out loud, even though we were in a courthouse, my father, already being upset, would have beat his ass and surely gone to jail.

Police were there as they would be in any court. It was quiet, and the room smelled like an old attic. The floors creaked as we walked to the stand. To me, the scene was set for someone to be massacred, taken to jail, or even have their head cut off. It was very intimidating, and I hated it.

As I looked up at the judge, all I could imagine was the movie *Roots*. In my mind, I could hear horses racing, and see white men riding the horses with guns slinging from their bodies, a cross burning in the front yard. Men yelled, "Come out, nigger, or we'll burn your house down. Come out, nigger, and bring the black nigger lady and kids with you."

That was all I could think about as we approached that large desk and the huge, thick white man standing there with his piercing cold blue eyes. I thought his mind was already made up. My sister and I would be split up, sent off to another family again. The closer we got to the huge wooden desk, the more I envisioned a white man with a sheet hood over his face, and nigger hater revealed in his eyes.

I grew angrier and angrier. I clutched my sister's hand, grabbed my father's coveralls, and cried intensely.

The judge pounded on the stand and yelled, "Who do you want to live with?"

"Both of my parents!" I said. I looked at my father and shivered in fear while tears rolled down my face.

My sister was quiet. Neither she nor I wanted to choose, but we both knew that my mother didn't want us. She was living in a one-bedroom apartment where she couldn't take care of us.

He then asked again, "Who do you want to live with?" He banged on the table.

I pissed my pants and yelled, "Both of my parents!"

"You can't," he said. "They're divorced. Now make a decision, or off you go to foster care."

As I made my decision to live with my father, I felt an extreme amount of relief. My sister made the same decision. We signed the paperwork, and off we went.

Before we left the courthouse, the big white man called my father and us back. "Mr. Walker," he said, "you have three weeks to get your house together. The social worker will be there to inspect, and if the house isn't ready for your kids to stay there, they will be given to the next foster parents who are eligible—or better yet, they'll be sent to an orphanage."

My eyes opened wide. I felt bad for my father. He had to let this man talk to him like that, just like in *Roots*. The man of the house was treated like shit, talked to in a very disrespectful way, and I hated it.

I asked my father, "Dad, is the house ready?"

He whispered, "No, but it will be, I think."

My father took us back to my mother's apartment. We stayed there for a few days, and then he came back to pick us up. As the Monte Carlo pulled up to get us, I saw my father and another person get out. It was my brother Ralph. He was tall, had big country sideburns still, and was dark as hell, even darker than when I first met him. I smiled hard while tears filled my eyes. I hadn't seen him in a while. Off we went to Seventieth Street and Hough, back to where it all started—the ghetto, by far the worst ghetto in Ohio. Hough was ranked amongst the worst neighborhoods in the world.

I heard dogs barking as we walked up to the house, which looked extremely spooky to me. Actually, it wasn't really a house. It was an apartment that was joined with another apartment—my uncle's place—the uncle who had knocked my mother's teeth out. The front windows had that ghetto plastic, and there was chicken wire on the windows. We walked around the back and headed inside. The rooms were blazing hot as there wasn't any air conditioning. In addition to roaches and rats, there was one bedroom, a kitchen with walls full of grease, and one small living room. The living room was probably ten feet by ten feet or maybe smaller. It was like being in a jail cell again. For some reason, despite all of this, I felt safe there, right in the middle of the ghetto. This was home. Even though it was dirty as hell, we knew that we would be taken care of. We were back with my father. The living conditions sucked, but it was a start.

We lived there for about a year. Remember, there was only one bedroom and one bed for four people. My father slept in the bed, and the rest of us slept on red velvet couches. The couches sucked, too. They were hard, full of dog hair, and smelled like dogs.

After we had gone back and forth from my mother's place to my father's place for about three weeks, it was time for the social worker to come and inspect the apartment. How could we sell her that this apartment was livable when it wasn't? The heat was off, it was wintertime, we had four people in there, and there was only one bed.

To solve the problem, my father and uncles came up with a great idea. Before the social worker came, they opened the door from our apartment and took it off the hinges so that it looked like a long hallway. My uncle left his apartment for a few hours so that we could act as if it was part of ours. My other uncle brought over a serious heater. It was kerosene, and we lit it in the house about three hours before the social worker arrived. The flame on that thing was huge. You could smell kerosene everywhere, but it surely warmed the apartment up.

Finally, the social worker arrived. She was a nice-looking black lady. My sister and I giggled as she spoke to us until my father gave us the death stare. That shut us the hell up pretty quick. We walked her into the house. It smelled like a huge gas station, but our trick worked. She walked through, and we pointed out each bedroom—now there were two—and we showed her my uncle's nice furniture in addition to our own dirty-ass red couches. For some reason, she bought off on it. I was amazed.

As she left, she looked back at my father and said, "'Bye, Zeke."

That was what they called my father in the hood. I knew then that they knew each other, and she had probably liked him. Whatever her reasoning, we were happy. My father signed the paperwork, and my sister and I finally knew for certain that we were not going to any orphanage or foster family.

I wouldn't be sleeping on the floor again, either. Even though I slept on that dirty, stinky velvet furniture for about a year, we were happy for once. The house was big, but it had five apartments upstairs and ours downstairs—crazy how it was put together.

Upstairs lived Willie Lee. He liked young girls, and they liked him. He paid them, and they took care of him sexually. Across from him was Mrs. Bernice. She was about six feet three inches and kept her hair nice, but all of her teeth were gone. I guess that was why she kept a man upstairs. You could hear her having sex all night. It sounded like they were tearing her house up, and we listened all the time.

Seventieth Street and Hough is where I learned all of my street knowledge—started playing pool, smoking, shooting dice, and flirting with the local prostitutes. It was a street filled with anything you could ask for. After-hours joints were all over. The adults had sex it seemed like every hour at these places, and kids stayed up all night. You could hear music all night, and the police never came. Hell, the Cleveland police only came over to Seventieth and Hough to buy cheap liquor and get sex, just like everybody else. They got their services free, a payoff for not reporting the illegal activities that were going on.

I played pool day and night, played so much that I started beating grown men, even at the age of twelve to fourteen. There weren't any trophies for me, but there were cash prizes and beer for me to win. I didn't drink the beer but won it for my father. I loved living over there. It shaped me into a man, good and bad.

At any time, you would see husbands and wives or boyfriends and girlfriends fighting, and these were violent fights. We had become numb to seeing this. I knew poverty quite well, and to this day, I'm extremely appreciative of that experience. It was all a part of life while living on Hough.

One of the after-hours joint owners was married. A very cool dude, rough-looking, he smoked big cigars and always flashed his money. He was tall and dark, but the ladies loved him. Really cool to the kids over there as well, he always gave us money to get lost when his girlfriend was around. It worked, of course. Although he was married with three or four kids, he had a much younger girlfriend. I believe he was in his fifties or sixties at the time, and she had to be in her late twenties. A very pretty lady with thick, round buttocks, she kept her hair done and had a beautiful smile.

One day, his wife and girlfriend had an encounter, and an argument ensued. His girlfriend went to her car, retrieved her gun, came back, and shot his wife. His wife died, and his girlfriend never went to jail for it. That was a sad day because on Seventieth and Hough, everyone was very close.

Hough was full of great fighters. Everyone on Hough could fight, and even to this day, if you ask a guy where he's from, once he says, "Hough," people will go the other way. The women could fight, too.

CHAPTER 26

Dark, Sexy Addict

**I knew he was getting high,
but I didn't know which drug
I would soon find out**

"YOU SHOULD LEARN how to box, Doubleo," Darryl, better known as Smokey, said. "Man, I used to whip ass in da joint."

Another early mentor of mine, he helped me get into boxing. He was quite dangerous. An older cat who had just come home from doing fifteen to twenty years for murder, he was scary, and intimidating. The women called him "Sexy Black." He was cool as hell and walked with serious confidence. The ladies adored him, but he didn't give a shit about that.

Smokey stood six feet tall and weighed about 190 pounds, muscles everywhere. He was built like a black chiseled statue. He wore a black Dobb hat, tilted to the side, with a stocking cap made from panty hose on his head, under the hat. He was not to be played with, but he looked out for the kids in our neighborhood. Bowlegged, he smoked Kool cigarettes and sported a permanent scowl on his face. His every word was delivered with a deep, scruffy voice, always convincing as he spoke. On the right side of his face was a scar, about ten inches long, one he received in a prison fight.

He always wore jeans that fit or slacks made by the tailors in downtown Cleveland on Fourth Street and cutoff shirts, the tank tops we now call wife-beaters. He surely didn't beat women, but he sure as hell beat men. When Smokey spoke, everyone listened. He was never wrong, either, even when he *was* wrong. We knew not to say shit about it, nor correct him. When we played cards on the porch, if he thought a woman spoke out of place, he just stared at her, and she'd shut up quick. When my friends and I saw this, we'd laugh.

"What the hell y'all laughing at, little boys?" one woman said once.

Smokey slowly cut his eyes at her, leaned down, grabbed the back of her neck, whispered in her ear, straightened up, and continued doing what he was doing. She then sat there extremely quiet and didn't move until he told her she could. She could have sat there for hours. As brutal as this was, we admired it.

Smokey liked to play spades. I was okay at it, so he asked me to be his partner. I had to play better because we didn't want to let Smokey down, regardless of what we were playing, and he hated losing.

Summertime in the '70s on Hough was full of everything. Each Friday night or Saturday afternoon, we would shoot pool or play card games, and there was plenty of liquor for the adults. One day, while on the porch playing spades, the game was a bit long, and I could see Smokey getting antsy, fidgeting in his seat, scratching his arms, jaw, and neck. I had no idea why, but he was moving in his chair, too, tapping his shoes on the floor, impatient. Really weird.

We were on the porch on Seventieth Street, between Hough and Chester. The music was loud. Lots of R&B was playing:

Smokey Robinson, the Temptations, the O'Jays, sounding really good.

A resident peeped his head out a window and yelled, "Turn that damn music down, y'all." He was a tenant in the house, a house that held about five additional people, some from jail, some just needing somewhere to live.

Smokey looked up at the window and yelled back, "Fuck you."

The man disappeared back into his room.

"Come on, man, play yo damn cards, Doubleo. Quit bullshittin'." Smokey stared at me, head slightly tilted down. He wasn't the same that day.

Our eyes met. He'd never talked to me that way, so I got nervous and played whatever was in my hand. I played the wrong card.

"Come on, boy, watch the damn cards being played. Fuck it, man. I quit. I'll be back." Smokey threw down his cards and got up from the table.

I felt relieved that he was gone. I didn't want to piss him off. He was fresh out of prison, and he had me by some fifteen years.

The rest of us sat there for about five minutes, then fifteen, then twenty. Suddenly, his grandmother Mildred came outside. Mildred was an even five feet tall, weighed a tad over a hundred pounds, wore a colorful scarf on her small head, and smoked Pall Mall cigarettes. A sundress draped her small body, and thick, cracked, smeared glasses sat on top of her head. Mildred was always the loudest on the porch. I never knew why she talked so much. She didn't have a tooth in her mouth, not one single tooth. Without teeth, when she smiled, it really seemed like her smile went from ear to ear . . . literally.

She'd talk or yell, and I could barely understand what she was saying with that Pall Mall cigarette stuck in the corner of her mouth, bouncing around with each word, and her tongue slashed around in her mouth, uncontrollably bumping up against her gums. Trying her best to pronounce each word, she really struggled, slobbering everywhere. "Doubleo, can you guys go up and check on Smokey?"

"Yes, ma'am," we responded. "We sure can."

We ran upstairs and knocked on the bathroom door a few times, then a few more times, with no response.

"Yo, man," I said to Tommy, "what do you think is wrong?"

"I don't know," he responded, "but we need to get in there."

We kicked the door in. Smokey was hunched over in the tub, the top part of his body submerged under the water.

"Damn, man, this don't look good," I said. "You grab one shoulder, and I'll grab the other one."

"Okay, cool," Tommy said anxiously.

We struggled to pull Smokey from the tub full of water.

"Lay him on his back, man, quickly," I demanded.

We lay Smokey down on his back.

"Look, man," Tommy said, "a damn needle."

We found a needle stuck in his right arm and a belt, pulled tight, on his left arm.

"Noooo, my baby," Mildred shouted as she burst into the bathroom. "Smokey, please don't leave me. Please don't leave me, baby."

An older gentleman living in the house heard the commotion. He burst out of his room, smelling like weed and beer. "Watch out, young man," he yelled. "Let me try to revive him." He started CPR, but it wasn't helping.

"Pump the water out," I said. "Keep going, please."

The older gentleman got tired. "Shit, this ain't working." He stood up, took a small breath, and tried again. "Man, I think we lost him." He was looking down at Smokey, lying on the floor, motionless.

I looked up at him.

"Damn," he mumbled while catching his breath. "That brown shit in that needle looks like heroin."

Tommy and I were holding Smokey by his shoulders. We were soaking wet from the water in the tub.

"Call the damn police," Mildred shouted. "Somebody please call the police." Tears ran down her face and dripped from her chin. "Please, please, baby, don't leave me."

I had wanted to be like Smokey so bad. He was strongly built, with jailhouse muscles, and had a strong hold on the women in the area. He knew how to fight and was respected by all. Men like Smokey were our role models, sadly.

Smokey wasn't breathing at all. It was too late. He died in our arms from a heroin overdose. My buddy was gone. I had lost my mentor. He taught me a lot.

* * *

We moved again, this time to the next street over. We were now on Seventy-First and Hough, just as ghetto as Seventieth Street. Life was okay. We were getting older, but the neighbors were becoming rougher. Our entire household was pretty popular, thanks to my father. Everyone in the neighborhood knew him, so we had no choice. We were involved in everything. My father played softball, my brother played football for East High, and I played football for Shaw High, wrestled for a time, and also boxed. At first, boxing looked scary to me. I watched it on TV, and my father and one of my uncles were boxers. My dad, as well as Smokey, got me into it, too. My father's brother—the uncle who knocked my mother's teeth out—wasn't a boxer, but as he'd proved, he could become violent.

I lost my first wrestling match in the ninth grade, and that was fine by me. I quit wrestling after that. Boxing was my love. Being a natural southpaw, fighting me was weird for other boxers, so they taught me how to fight ambidextrously, and this was an advantage for me. I would walk from home to the gym and back every day, about three miles each way, but I loved it. I didn't love getting my ass kicked every day, but boxing stopped everyone from messing with me, and it gave me confidence.

At my gym on Fifty-Fifth and Lexington, we would spar every day, and it didn't matter what weight class you were in; you would spar the professionals. It made you tough really quick. I've had my share of busted lips and puffy and swollen eyes. That was what made me learn and sharpen my defense. You learn quick when you have an older professional guy all over you like that. Some of the worst punches I took were to the stomach, kidneys, nose, and jaw, but by far the worst was getting hit in my lower jaw with my mouth open. That would make most people quit on the spot, but I never did. I hung in there.

My trainer was a well-known boxer back in the '60s and '70s. By the time he was training me, he had ballooned up to about three hundred pounds, but he could still fight. What was strange to me while boxing at the gym was that he walked around naked all the time, even while yelling at me when I was sparring. It was hard to look in my corner for help when I was getting my ass kicked, and my trainer was naked with his balls hanging out. It was just hard to concentrate. I mean, he was butt-ass naked. When the bell rang for the end of my round, I would rather keep getting my ass kicked than go back to my corner. I would stand in the center of the ring after the bell, and he'd call me over as he walked away, his chunky ass showing, as he wore nothing more than a jock strap. He was so fat that you couldn't even see the straps.

I boxed for a few years, enough to learn some self-defense, and then moved on.

My sister was never a boxer, but man, she was tough. Since she grew up with all men and boys around, she had to be. Even when she was young, her male friends were little hustlers. They stole and sold clothes, jewelry, and cars. It benefitted me because they had stuff for me to buy. Pretty cool dudes, some of them, even to this day. My sister and I were tight, but we fought all the time growing up. I guess it was a sibling thing. Me fighting her all the time must have continued on into her high school days, and it helped her.

I remember coming home one day to see my father talking to my sister. I overheard him saying, "Why the hell did you get suspended?"

She had gotten into a fight. Little did I know it was that and more. The girl she hit was pretty nice-looking, but not after my sister laid hands on her. My sister was very strong, with solid natural muscles. She even gave me a hard time when we were fighting. This young lady did something to my sister that set her off for some reason. The fight ensued, and my sister punched the girl in the eye. My father had to go to the school and see the pictures. The young lady's eye was closed shut. I had never seen a girl hit another girl and have those results. My sister had never had any problems in school, but after that right hook, she was surely one to reckon with.

* * *

Summer soon came back around, and during the summers on Seventy-First Street, we had a blast. I had a bed for the first time in years, my sister had a bed, and my father slept in the lady's house in back of us.

As you probably know, Cleveland is hot in the summer. It's hot as hell, people are mad, and they drink. My father, silly as he was, came up with the great idea of stealing a fire hydrant wrench and opening the hydrant as wide as he could to allow the water to flow freely. It was a free-for-all. Everyone came out to cool off—men with perms, little kids, dogs, even the women with those big pink rollers. Everyone from our community was there having fun—athletes, hustlers, gangsters, drug addicts, prostitutes, gay men, gay women. Our neighborhood had it all, and this was one thing that brought us all together.

My father had a few cars during that time. One car that everyone loved was his beige LeBaron. It had a nice radio, thick whitewall tires, and he kept it clean. I was only fifteen, but I could already drive, and downtown Cleveland was only twenty minutes from our house. I had my eye on that car! I learned to drive early from my father and my cousins. I became a better driver when my cousins stole a Cleveland police car. It wasn't your average cop car. It was loaded down and unmarked, but it had some nice stuff in it. They stole it from downtown Cleveland, and we went joyriding for a while.

This wasn't unusual for us at all. Kids in my neighborhood stole cars all the time. The grown men taught us how to do it with just a pair of pliers or a screwdriver on the starter posts. After stealing the car, we'd joyride for a few hours—even days— until we tired of it and then leave the car in some abandoned parking lot like it was no big deal. Later, someone else would come by, jack the car up, put it on cement blocks, and take the tires and radio (the seats, too, if they were leather).

This gave me confidence—enough confidence that when my father would work the graveyard shift at Ford Motor Company, I would steal his beige LeBaron and drive downtown to meet the prostitutes. In a way, I was stealing his car, but I had the keys. Had he known what I was up to, I would've gotten my ass beat for sure.

He eventually figured it out. One day, when he left for work, he took the battery out without me knowing. He'd had an idea that I had been taking the car because I wasn't being careful enough to park it the right way when I brought it back. That day, I tried to start the car, but the engine wouldn't turn over. I knew there wasn't a battery in there, so I went to my uncle's car, took his battery, and got my dad's car up and running again. I had failed to notice that my father had also removed his license plate, though. It wasn't long before the police were following me, and pulled me over.

I was lucky that they let me go, considering that I was only fifteen at the time. Needless to say, that was the last time I stole my father's car. Of course, driving at fifteen was hardly as bad as the fact that I was driving downtown to meet the prostitutes. I didn't tell anyone, not even my siblings. I never took any of my friends down there, either.

I had my first encounter with a prostitute at fifteen. It was scary but exciting at the same time. Driving down Prospect Avenue in downtown Cleveland, you could get anything you wanted: weed, cocaine, sex, porn. Whatever you wanted, it was there. I cruised down Euclid Avenue, turned left on Ninth Street, and headed to my destination: Prospect, around Fourth Avenue. I immediately saw a woman who caught my eye. She was slowly strutting, shaking her ass, really twisting her hips in a provocative way. That made my heart pump faster. My music in the car was playing loud. The Temptations crooned, "Ain't too Proud to Beg," ironically. I reduced my speed to get the woman's attention.

She got mine first. "Psssst," the lady called out.

My windows were down. I lowered the music. Playing old-school music made me seem older than I was, and it worked every time. I gently pulled over to the curb. "What's up?" I asked her.

"Hey, baby," she responded, leaning into the car window while smoking a cigarette. "You looking for a good time?" She took a drag, blowing the smoke into my car.

"Hell, yeah," I responded. "What's up? How much?" I made my voice deeper to seem older.

"Well, for you, ass, a hundred dollars. Head, you can gimme twenty dollars."

"Cool," I responded. "Hop in."

"You're cute," she said.

"Thanks. You are, too."

She rubbed my right thigh, and I rubbed hers.

"Where you wanna go?" I asked her.

"Turn right here. You see that blue dumpster? Go behind that and turn the car and lights off."

Her name was Carmel. I'm sure that was a made-up name, but I didn't care. Hell, my name was Romeo while I was downtown.

Carmel was very pretty, with short, thick thighs, curly hair, long eyelashes, and full lips. I knew then it was going to feel good, and it did.

"So, what you want, young man?" she asked. "Some head? You cool with that?"

"Hell, yeah."

"Yeah," she replied. "I'm tryin' to get paid, not make love."

I immediately got excited. My palms were sweating, my heart pounding. All of my childhood thoughts of being molested started running through my head. Her lips, her pretty skin, her beautiful hair—those reminders all came *right* back. As strange as it may seem, I felt like I was being molested again, but this time, I had more control.

We went behind an adult bookstore next to an old blue dumpster, and she got started on me. I was breathing hard, the windows were fogged, and at this point, nothing mattered. Most, if not all, prostitutes would just get in the car with me. Hell, they didn't care how old I was. I had a car, so I guess in their minds, I was old enough. My demons were in full swing. I didn't have a license and wasn't legal to drive, but my damaged soul needed to be fed, and it was, quite often. Carmel was my motivation to work. I saved my money to see her almost every Friday or Saturday that summer. I was addicted to her.

"See you next week, Romeo," she said as she smiled and walked away with that same provocative, hip-swinging walk. She had another job to do.

Stealing cars, seeing prostitutes—yes, not normal things for most young teenagers to do, but I was growing up in a world where these kinds of things were normal. I'll never forget the night I heard my father and his friends talking about their friend who had robbed a bank. I was lying down in my bedroom, but I knew they were huddled up in the living room because I could hear them through the thin walls.

"Yo, Zeke, you hear about Bo-bo?"

"Nah, man. What's up?"

I knew Bo-bo. He used to come over and play with us. He was scary-looking, tall and dark, with lots of bumps on his face. He looked like a monster.

"Man, that crazy nigga robbed a bank."

"He did *what*?" I could hear my father's surprised voice through the wall.

"You heard me. He robbed a bank, and the Cleveland police are looking for him now. He got away with over twenty thousand dollars."

"Shit, man. I need some of that. Where's the money?"

It turned out that nobody knew where Bo-bo was. He was eventually caught, but they never recovered the money, and he went to prison for twelve years.

I think back on times like these and wonder how it is that I made it out of that life without going down the same miserable path of so many of the others I knew. During my time growing up, I saw a lot, encountered many things, and participated in quite a few of them. I had the perfect blueprint to become a pimp, whoremonger, hustler, murderer, or bank robber. I saw it all at a very early age, so young that much of it even impressed me. For some reason, though, and I can't explain this, I chose not to go down that path. God had me all along. He surely did, and that's why I love him.

CHAPTER 27

Dark Love

AT FIFTEEN, I fell in love with my first dark-skinned lady. She was twenty-one. Her skin was smooth, and she sported plump lips—the ones I'd always liked on my babysitter—a nice booty, and very nice and round titties. We'll call her Lisa. Lisa was cool. She played *Pac-Man* better than anyone else in the neighborhood, popped her gum loud as hell, and smoked Newports. Although she was pretty, at least to me, she had a bad grade of hair. The top of her head usually looked nice, but the back was full of naps. I didn't care, though. She did have a beautiful personality, and that, among other things, drew me to her. This was my first real crush after my brief affair with my babysitter at nine years old.

Of all those lovely women on Hough, Lisa would never give me the time of day. That all changed one day when Lisa was outside with my sister, sitting between my sister's legs on the stairs of the apartment, getting her hair braided. Back then, it was nothing to see women getting their hair done outside—braids, perms, hot combs, Sulfur 8—they did it all outside.

I was so attracted to Lisa, it was insane. She was still a virgin, my sister told me. I knew that I had more experience than she did, so I was ready. Anyway, as I came outside, I saw Lisa and my sister sitting there. I sat down, and she turned her head slightly to the right. For some odd reason, I noticed her thick lips from where I was sitting. My mind quickly went back to a vision of my babysitter's lips. That didn't help me any. Actually, it made it worse. I got excited.

I sat there on those cement stairs and waited until my penis got extremely hard. I was sitting three or four stairs up from her, and gently eased down and then grabbed her hand to place it on my penis. She touched it, then looked me directly in the eyes. When she didn't smile, I became afraid.

Oh shit, I thought, am *I being disrespectful?*

Then I saw a look in her eyes that made me think she wanted me. It was that same look that my babysitter gave me. Immediately, my demons came back into my life, along with the feeling I experienced when playing house.

Another woman older than I am that I'm attracted to, I thought.

I couldn't control it, even if I tried to. The feeling was just too strong to push out of my mind.

Lisa never said anything to me. I sat there, and she held my penis for what seemed like an eternity. My sister had no clue. As darkness crept in, my sister finished her hair, and Lisa got up. I asked her to follow me down to Nia's house. Nia was only fourteen, but she had a place of her own, given to her by Mr. Green, who was known to give money to the teenage girls in our neighborhood if they would let him lick and fondle them. Everyone in the neighborhood knew he was doing this, but he was also giving their mothers money, so no one ever said anything. He was a pure sugar daddy, and it actually helped me that night.

I walked Lisa down the street, and we went into Nia's house and made out for hours. I loved it. This was my first time being with a dark-skinned grown woman, and this was also my first time sucking titties.

After being with Lisa for a month or so, I met a young lady named Patrice.

CHAPTER 28
My Girlfriend Died

PATRICE WAS TOP-HEAVY and had nice lips. I played football and softball at Martin Luther King Jr. High School, so she knew me from that. She was popular in the neighborhood, and so was I. I had my mother's hair. It was wavy, with the best waves in the neighborhood and in high school.

I was at the corner store one night when Patrice approached me. Patrice and I kissed, played, and talked often for almost a year. During the summer, Patrice and I hung out. We walked around, ate candy, laughed, and kissed. We were a very cool and tight couple. I really enjoyed Patrice, and she enjoyed me, as well.

One day when I was at Patrice's house, she said she wasn't feeling well. Neither one of us knew what was going on, but we knew something was bad. This was the day she had promised to have sex with me, but she was in intense pain and sex wasn't going to happen. She told her mother and brother, and she was ultimately taken to the hospital. Not long after arriving there, Patrice was diagnosed with cancer. She didn't live through the summer. She was really my first girlfriend, and she died of cancer at fifteen years old.

I was devastated. For a while, I couldn't function. I was hurt. I didn't want to play sports. All I wanted to do was visit with her family.

I didn't want to be with anyone again until I met Sasha.

CHAPTER 29

Painful Sex in My Father's Car

**This place scared me forever
The word "FREE" comes at a cost**

I T WAS HOT, all right. Sasha was young, sexy, curvy, and extremely sexually active. I was again at the corner store playing Pac-Man when Sasha walked in. I looked at her, she looked at me, and I instantly got hard. She had a body like Lisa's, and I couldn't resist. She was with her girlfriend, and her girl was down, too.

I went to get my boy. His name was Terry, and he was seventeen. A cool, slim dude, he worked on cars and always had one to drive. That day, however, his father wouldn't let him get the car, so I planned to take my father's car later that night while he was at work. After dark, I grabbed the keys to the LeBaron, picked up my boy, went to get Sasha and her girl, and we all had sex in my father's car. It was all four of us in there—me and Sasha in the back, and my boy and her girl in the front.

Terry drove the car out to the lake. Lake Erie was the place where everyone went to have sex outside in the park on the grass or in the car. This was the first time that a girl rode me, and I loved it. Sasha was very sexy. The problem was that she was the ex-girlfriend of a guy in the hood, and once he found out that I'd had sex with her, he was pissed. Little did he know, he wasn't as pissed as I was after I had sex with Sasha. This was my first time having sex in a car, my first time having a girl ride me, but the pleasantry wouldn't last long.

We left Lake Erie and dropped Sasha and her girl off at home. "See y'all later," we told them. "Thanks for a great time."

"Man, old girl felt good, like real good," I told Terry.

"Yeah, her girl did, too,"

We laughed and drove away. Three days later, I headed to work. I took the bus most times, so I stopped at the store, grabbed some chips and a juice, and hopped on the bus. I was about forty-five minutes from work, so by the time I got there, I had to pee. I hopped off the bus, went into work, and stopped at the bathroom first. I started to pee, and a horrific burning sensation came from my penis. A white, yellowish discharge followed. My knees buckled, and I grabbed the pipes above the urinal to hold on to for dear life. I clenched my butt cheeks and tried to pee again, slowly. It didn't work. The burning felt like someone had cut me wide open and poured hot sauce on my penis.

"Ahhh," I yelled out.

My boss busted in the door. "Leon, are you okay? What's wrong?"

"Nooo, man, I'm not okay. I don't know what's wrong. My penis burns bad, like really bad, and I want to stop peeing, but I can't."

"Get it all out," he said, chuckling. "Uh-oh, buddy, sounds like you might have a disease."

"A disease, like what kind, Mr. Nelson?"

"Hell, I don't know. There's plenty to go around. Sounds like you got a hot one." He chuckled again. "Either way, you need to get checked, my friend."

"Damn, I can't tell my father about this. I just can't."

"Well, its better to get checked than to have your little peter fall off," he said.

"Yeah, you're right."

My boss was a cool older white guy. Mr. Nelson was his name. He was about sixty years old at the time, walked with a cane, and had gray hair and a pudgy red nose.

I tried to stop peeing but couldn't. I peed every few seconds, trying to end it, but the juice I had drunk just kept coming out, and I kept burning and leaking. That shit hurt like hell. I had no idea what to do. I didn't want to tell anyone. I was terrified, and I didn't even tell Sasha. I was pissed, sick, and in pain.

I headed home for the day. As I got on Seventy-First and Hough, I saw Don, an older friend I trusted in the neighborhood.

I decided to ask him for advice. "Yo, man," I said, "have you ever taken a piss, and your dick just burned?"

"Oh hell, yeah, man. All the girls I sleep with, not sure who, but one of them gave me gonorrhea."

"What? How did it feel, man?"

"Well, when I went to take a piss, it burned like hell. Are you burnin', man?"

"Hell, yeah, and I . . ."

He cut me off. "What about dripping?"

"Yeah, that too, man. When I woke up, my dick was stuck to my underwear."

"You got it, buddy. You might have gonorrhea."

"What can I do?" I asked him.

"Well, to keep it on the low, go to the free clinic. It's on

Euclid, by the cemetery. They'll check you out, then treat you if you have it, but I'm sure you do."

Not long after we talked, I caught the #6 bus and headed to the free clinic. As I went in, the burning started again. I grabbed my pants tightly, squirming as I tried to focus on the young woman in front of me.

"How can I help you, young man?" she asked me. "Looks like you need to see the doctor."

She was pretty, with a slim build, long hair, and nice lips. Just my luck.

"Well, I'm, I'm . . ."

She cut me off. "You're burning, huh?"

"Yeah, and dripping, too."

"Okay, hold on. Let me get the doctor. Have a seat."

I sat there for about thirty minutes, burning and twitching in my pants. Next to me was a room with brown curtains all around it, a stool, and the doctor's needles.

All of a sudden, I heard the doctor say, "Now this is gonna hurt. Take your pants down and bend over."

I was ready to run right out of the place when I heard that.

"Ahhh!" a man screamed. "Doc, Doc, no. Take it out, please!"

My heart pounding. *Damn it*, I thought, *I'm next.*

The man burst out from behind the curtains, holding his ass and limping.

"Keep walking," the doctor said, "and try to sit on your butt and roll around some. That'll make the medicine go into your bloodstream faster."

"Okay, Doc, I will," the man replied.

As he walked by me, I asked him, "Hey, man, how long is the needle?"

He said the needle wasn't too bad, but asked me, "Do you see that long, thin metal thing right there?" He pointed to the doctor's table.

"Yeah, I see it. What's that?"

"Well, he's going to slowly push that down into your penis."

"What!" I yelled. "No way, man. It's too long. It'll go into my back through my penis."

"Yeah, that's about how it's gonna feel," he said.

"Fuck." I sat there, fists balled up, lips dry, and legs crossed.

"Go ahead, man, go on in there."

I went in and waited for the doctor in the small, closed-off room. The curtains swung back, and the doctor, glasses on top of his head, entered. The room was quiet. He sterilized the long metal thing. It looked like a needle, but it wasn't sharp, and it had a small loop at the end of it.

He sat down and swung his smock back. "Give it here," he said. "Gimme your penis. I need to go in ya to get the mucus out." He lowered his glasses onto his face and leaned in, slowly and painfully sliding the metal rod into my penis.

I held my breath and watched it disappear into my body. He kept sliding it in. *Will it touch my spine?* I wondered. My head and face were full of sweat, and my body was stiff. I bit down, keeping my mouth closed tight.

"Okay, got it, young man. There's a lot of mucus here. Let me run a quick test. Be right back." He left the room. About an hour later, the curtains swooshed open. "Yep, you got it, buddy."

"What's that, Doc?" I asked.

"You have gonorrhea, and it's pretty bad. Okay, now turn around. You need two shots in your butt."

I hated needles. They scared the hell out of me. "Doc, can I just take pills?"

"Oh yeah, you sure can."

"Whew." I sighed in relief.

Then he said, "I'll give you those, too. Now bend over."

I bent over. Gently laying my head on the cold steel stool for comfort, I took a deep breath.

Doc sat down, swung open the small refrigerator, and pulled out a little bottle of medicine.

"What's that, Doc?" I asked.

"Penicillin. We keep it cold. It's pretty thick, so this will be the painful part. You're gonna feel it go into your butt muscles. As the medicine enters, it'll feel like it's spreading the muscles apart, so *don't move*." He spoke in a low, serious voice. "If you move, the needle will lacerate your ass. Loosen your butt cheeks, buddy, loosen up, so I get it all in ya. Don't get scared now. You weren't scared when you were having sex, were ya?"

"I was, Doc, and excited, too," I replied.

"Stop shakin'. It'll be over pretty quick." Slowly, he aimed the sharp, thin needle at my butt.

Ready to scream, I peeked back, mouth open, hands and forehead pumping sweat. Suddenly, I felt a sharp pinch in one butt cheek. I grunted in pain. "Doc, that hurts," I moaned through my teeth. "Can we take a break?"

"I'm sure it doesn't hurt like the burning in your penis. Now swing over some. You need two shots." He shoved my butt over to get a clear shot in the other cheek.

I felt another pinch, then felt the cold, thick medicine enter my other butt cheek.

"We're done. You have some blood on your cheeks. I'll put some gauze and Band-Aids on them for ya."

I lifted my head off the cold chair, my mouth closed tightly. "Mmm, Doc." I shook my head, and a tear rolled down my face.

"Here, wipe your head, young man. I see this was pretty traumatic for ya."

"Yeah it was, Doc. It really was."

"Take it easy, young man. Take it easy, and don't come back."

"I won't, Doc. I surely won't." I limped out of the free clinic and caught the #6 bus back home.

"Hey, young man," a lady called out, "you wanna seat?"

"No, ma'am, I'm good." I stood all the way home. Now both my ass and penis were hurting badly. What a horrible day!

CHAPTER 30

Hood Shit—Heroin—
That Knife

B Y THIS POINT, things in my life were starting to feel a bit calmer. I was feeling much better about my parents' divorce. We were living in my father's new two-bedroom house. The kitchen and bathroom were small, but it was still better than the other house on Seventieth and Hough. Still kids everywhere, still dogs barking, so not much had changed in that regard, but the house was so much cleaner and better. My sister had a bedroom, and my brother slept on the couch. My father either slept on the other couch or with the women in the building.

Not that there still wasn't drama to contend with. Next door to us lived two transgender men—I don't know what they called themselves, maybe "transvestites," or words to that effect. They were both tall, had long hair, and had just gotten out of jail having done twenty years for murder. They were pretty cool, and they could fight. Both of them had five o'clock shadows, so we knew that they were men, but no one dared to call them out on it.

Hough was full of so many characters back then. Great fighters, hustlers, drug dealers, pimps, prostitutes, and gays. We all got along quite well, though. We had some regular folks, too, ones like Mrs. Bee, who lived right behind us. I used to go out our back door and right into her house. She was a cute little old lady with a huge butt. Her boyfriend, UNC, was about seventy years old, with gray hair and no teeth, and still smoked cigarettes. They were both cool. I used to help Mrs. Bee with whatever they needed help with, and she would give me fruit or some spare change.

My father eventually started working the graveyard shift again, which left me and my siblings with the freedom to do whatever we wanted from eleven p.m. until seven a.m. the next day. It was wonderful. We basically raised ourselves while he was off at work.

Don't get me wrong. We had a solid household and major respect for my father. But when he was at work, we let loose. My sister started me smoking weed. Her girlfriends would come by, and since I was sixteen and my sister was fifteen, we had weed, a car, and everyone in the apartment complex was sexually active. Weed makes you horny and hungry. It was really a great feeling.

I remember my sister's friend bringing over some weed one night. My father was gone, so we sat out on the porch and smoked for quite a while. Later that night, my uncle and cousin came over and joined us. By this time, we were nice and high. We walked to the store to get some Doritos, Snickers, and Entenmann's chocolate chip cookies. What a meal! They were my favorites, and the high was wonderful.

As my cousins rolled up, they got out of the car dressed like the Mod Squad with their hair all picked out, round dark glasses, and bell-bottom pants. They thought they were cute, but they were just wrong that day. You know if you've ever smoked weed that it makes everything funny, and we laughed hard as hell at those characters. We couldn't stop.

Well, they walked on past us and into the house. It was late, and my father was still at work. They were in there for a while before we went back inside to see if they were okay. They were locked in the bathroom, and we had no idea why, but they said they were fine, so we left it alone and went to sleep. By the time my father got home, my cousins were gone. He came into our room and woke us up. He wanted to know if we had been getting high. It turned out that my cousins had left lighters, spoons, and old needles in our bathroom. They had been freebasing and cooking cocaine and heroin.

One of those cousins was the same one who had been knocked out by my uncle. He had a girlfriend named Lidia, nice-looking, short, with good hair, a lovely body, and a great smile. They had to have been in their thirties at this point. Lidia was always nice to us when she came by with our cousin, but we didn't see her often because my cousin was married and did his business at my father's apartment on occasion.

Not long after my cousin and his mistress left our house one evening, we found out that he was in the hospital. We didn't know what happened but soon learned that Lidia had tried to kill him. She stabbed him upward of twenty-three times, mostly to his neck, jaw, and face. His jaw was wired shut, but he lived.

After that incident, I was terrified of small women. I thought they were all dangerous, probably because they were small, short, and didn't take anyone's shit. This would later catch up with me, as I actually would later date a small, short young lady and would pay the price for it.

CHAPTER 31

They called us Jungle Negros and Porch Monkeys

Throughout this period of our lives, we lived like animals, and we were okay with it. The neighborhood was a lot of fun, but that didn't come without a cost. There was also lots of drama, arguing, fighting, theft—you name it. We were all part of stealing something and watching people get shot. It was our own little hell filled with adrenaline and blood-pumping action.

One day my buddy, who was about five years older than me, decided that he wanted to do something crazy.

"Cool," I said. "What do you have in mind?"

"Let's rob the ice cream truck."

"What, are you serious?"

"Hell, yeah, man. It's hot, and we're broke and hungry."

"I'm in, man. Let's do it."

The day grew into night, and the sun was setting. We were hungry and ready for anything. Just then we heard the little ice cream truck slowly coming down the street, getting closer and closer. My friend and I looked at each other.

"Dub, are you ready?"

"Yep, you bet."

The truck pulled up, the man slid the door open, and we started to order even though we didn't have any money on us.

He leaned out of his little door, and just like that, my buddy grabbed him by the neck. "Don't move, motherfucker, or else," he whispered to him.

"Cut that damn music off," I demanded, my confidence high, my heart racing. I bit down on my teeth, watching the ice cream man, as my friend had his huge hands around his neck. We were really into it. I had to keep going through with the robbery. We didn't have time to back out.

Panicking, the driver turned around, bent over, and shut the music off. His voice cracking with fear, his hands trembling, he begged, "Please, don't hurt me." His face was dark, his eyes red, and he was sweating and shaking.

I could see tears start to slowly roll down his face, but I didn't even care. We wanted ice cream and money. That's all that was on our minds.

"I'm just trying to make a living and feed my family," he said. "Please don't hurt me."

At the time, I couldn't have cared less. As far as I was concerned, he was on Hough, so he should've known better. We proceeded to take all of his ice cream, empty his little cash register, and take off. We stole about eighty-five dollars, a lot back then.

Laughing and eating ice cream all night, we even had weed to smoke, so we were set. We sat outside while there was a party going on next door, with loud music, lots of people, and drugs— you name it. All of a sudden, two guys came tumbling out the door, wrestling, fighting, and arguing over a record album. The argument progressed, getting more and more intense, until one of the guys pulled out a gun—it looked like a .38 special—and shot the other guy directly in the head. He fell to the ground, and blood went everywhere.

Chaos ensued. We ran into each other trying to get away, and all we could see was the guy rolling around on the ground, bleeding and screaming. Then he just stopped. He died, right there in front of us. We were young—merely teenagers—and in shock. There was brain matter and blood all over the ground. It was horrendous. The police never picked up the killer, and in the hood, you had better not say a damn thing. We kept our mouths shut.

That wasn't the only time I saw a man with his head split open. One day, we had been playing football. The game was over, and we were on our way to the nearest corner store. As we walked, we heard screeching tires from a van. It turned the corner wildly. Most of us ran, but Pookie couldn't get out of the way in time. The van struck him and busted his head wide open. He landed on top of the van and rolled down and hit the ground, knocking out almost all of his teeth. He died later that day in the hospital, only sixteen years old.

I had another friend die the same way shortly thereafter. We were on a sports recruiting tour to a local school, and he was getting a ride down there when the car broke down on the freeway. The kids were just sitting there on the guardrail when a semi driving by lost its tire. It exploded, flying in the direction of my friends. Most of them scattered, but the tire hit another one of my buddies and killed him instantly. He, too, was only sixteen years old.

Looking back on the ice cream truck robbery, I've always felt bad over the years. What we did was wrong, and I will forever owe society for that. That man provided us with ice cream for years on Seventy-First and Hough, and we ruined his life. We never had an ice cream truck on Seventy-First and Hough ever again. Now I respect even more those who work hard and provide for their family. The vision of that man's face and his terrified look has never left me.

Still, at the time, we were so accustomed to the violence that it all seemed almost normal to us. It wasn't unusual for people on Hough to turn on each other, too.

One day in particular, we were hanging out, just chilling. I had a friend named Da-da. He was short, fat, and smoked cigarettes like a grown man. He was only fifteen, but he was about five feet seven and weighed 240 pounds. He smoked like a grown man, with a cigarette hanging from his mouth. It always amazed me how he could do that at such a young age. He wasn't tough, nor could he fight, but he was very abusive to his mother nonetheless.

One day, I went by his house to see if he could hang out. It was late, around ten p.m. I knocked, and he came to the door. "Yo, man, let's kick it," I said.

His mom immediately said no, and I started to walk away when I heard him turn to her and say, "Bitch, he ain't talking to you. Sit yo fat ass down."

I was shocked, but at the time, I laughed. It was wrong for him to say that to his mother, but he didn't care. He came out of the house, and we hit the block. Up came another buddy of mine. He and Da-da didn't get along, and this night, an argument broke out. Da-da couldn't fight, but when Moe slapped the shit out of him, he was quick to run into his house and then right back out with his father's huge shotgun. I yelled at Moe to leave, but he refused.

"Fuck that. He ain't gonna shoot me. I ain't goin' nowhere."

Da-da walked right up with the gun, and still Moe didn't move. I just knew Da-da was going to shoot him, so I took the gun and broke up the altercation. Da-da never forgot that day, and being bullied would later both help and hurt him. Back in 2008, I read about an incident involving Da-da. Some guys jumped him but didn't know that Da-da was known for having a gun. He shot the guys who jumped him and killed one of them. Da-da is now serving life in prison for murder.

*   *   *

I got older and wiser, having the time of my life in the ghetto. My father eventually found a house on Penrose. We called it the "Big Blue House." The house was located in East Cleveland, in a cool area with lots of teenagers our age—and lots of drama, too.

My father purchased it for a measly $2,500, and that meant that it needed a lot of work. It was a duplex and had missing shingles, broken windows, and missing doors. The grass had been torn up, and the bricks in the front lawn were broken or missing. Trash filled the backyard, dog mess was everywhere, there were no gutters, and the roof had a hole in it. It was just in bad shape. My father hired plumbers, painters, electricians, and other workmen to bring the house up to specifications.

I was happy as hell. Even though it was a shell of a house, things were getting better, and fast. Little did I know, my sister and I were the other workers who were going to be working on the house—but we weren't getting paid. I knew that I had a good work ethic—my mother started that—but I had no idea that it could be painful at times. As we visited the house each day, we'd walk through, look around, clean up, and see what else we could do that day before the sun went down. The electricity wasn't hooked up yet, nor was the water, so we thought there wasn't much we could do yet.

My father found plenty for us to do, though. The wooden banisters looked horrible, all beat-up, and they needed painting. He made us chip the old paint off of them. I thought

to myself that there was no way we could do that. They weren't
the rail kind. They were wooden and individually placed along
the front porch. There were about forty of them, and they were
old as hell. They'd been there for years, covered with paint and
whatever else the cold winters had brought. It took us months
to chip those things down to the bare wood. All of that work,
and later on, my father decided to go with metal banisters. Boy,
was I pissed, but do you think I said anything? Hell, no! We
had worked our asses off, and work was work. My father had
wanted it done, so we did it.

No matter what, we finally had a new house with a lot of
bedrooms, and we were excited. We chose which ones we
wanted for ourselves. Every time I rode the bus from our old
home on Hough to East Cleveland, it went by our new home. I
could see it from the street, and I'd look at it each time. It was
wonderful.

One of the other great things about this time in my life was
getting to know my older brother, the one from Alabama. He
became very instrumental in my life, and he came at just the
right time. I was young, the divorce had been devastating, and
he was strong and energetic. He protected me and my sister.
A country boy now living in the city—pretty cool. He played
football for East High School in Cleveland on a great team with
guys who ended up getting scholarships to Penn State, West
Virginia, and other Division I schools. Being from the country,
my brother wasn't very street savvy until he came to Cleveland.
Once he got there, all of that changed.

On the football team, he had a nickname—they called him
"Country," and that's what he was. After being there a while,
though, he became just like any other city boy. He started
drinking hard liquor, something he hadn't done back in
Alabama. One day, my brother got drunk, thinking he could
hang out late and just go into work drunk the next day. He

quickly found out that wasn't the case. My uncle had gotten him a job parking cars downtown, and that was where he and my father thought my brother was. Later that day, though, my uncle called my father because he couldn't find my brother. He had come to work, all right, but he had found himself a place to sleep off that hangover: in the back of a nice-ass Cadillac. He knew what he was doing—he surely found the right car.

The longer Country stayed in Cleveland, the more comfortable and street-smart he became. Sometimes, it got him in trouble with my father. Country could be a very nice guy until you pissed him off. From what I heard, this one time he had been selling belts at school, and one kid didn't want to pay him. In order to get the kid to pay up, he wouldn't let the kid out of a classroom. Finally, the kid tried to escape by climbing out the window and scaling the walls of the school. The school called my father, and my brother had hell to pay after that. He got suspended from school, first of all, and then when he got home, he was also punished by my father, who made him clean the house for hours, clean the cars, feed the dogs, clean dog shit, cut the grass. He literally got his ass worked off that day.

When my father was mad or disappointed, he would go to the extreme to punish you, and he could make you feel sorry without ever even putting hands on you. It was all mental, and this was where I learned my way of punishing my kids—quite extreme, but it worked. Things like this made my brother stay in school. He never got suspended again, and from watching this whole thing play out, neither did I. When my brother got older, and he left home to start a family of his own, I really missed him.

CHAPTER 32

Broomstick Broke Off Inside Her

It used to be a funeral home

It was known to have plenty of ghost

EVEN WITH THINGS going so well, trouble and drama could always find me. I was getting older, hanging out in the hood, having fun, and looking for ways to make money. For a lot of kids, that meant stealing clothes and selling them. It was definitely tempting, as my sister's friends were very good at it, often bringing clothing to my house to sell or even just to give her. This impressed me. These guys were about my age, or maybe a little bit older. All I could think of was that it was time for me to make some money, too.

There was a house a little ways down from us where fancy parties were held on the weekends. There were all sorts of cars parked in the back: Porsches, Cadillacs, Mercedes-Benzes, Rolls-Royces. You name it, the car was there. When darkness came, I would walk down there just to see who was pulling up, and what kind of cars were arriving. I'd see all sorts of celebrities, and I would wonder why they would come to our neighborhood with those nice cars. As I got closer to the house and cars, I could hear singing, laughing, and partying. Curious, I devised a plan to get into one of those parties.

It all started with a knock on the door. A short, brown-skinned lady answered the door. She had a small curly Afro, smooth brown skin, and thick arms. Her eyelids were a bit swollen, probably from lack of sleep. Her calves were full of muscles, and I could see the varicose veins running down her legs.

"How can I help you, little boy?" she asked. She was wearing a brown sundress, without a bra. Her titties were pretty low, and her nipples protruded through her dress.

She didn't seem to care, but I was sure looking. I leaned back, looked up at her, and responded, "Hi, I'm Doubleo, and I see that you have a lot of trash out here. Your grass needs to be cut, and I can also work inside if you'll allow me."

"Are you Zeke's son?" she asked.

"Yes," I responded, and she invited me in.

I walked back home after observing for hours, went to sleep, and then the next day, I found the courage to knock on the door again. The house was huge. I saw that there was weed, cocaine, and liquor everywhere.

We sat down and talked out a plan. Then she hired me to be her little housekeeper. In the middle of the conversation, she turned and snorted a long line of cocaine, right in front of me.

"Now," she said, "if you're going to work here, keep ya damn mouth shut."

"No problem," I said, "but you have some cocaine on your nose still . . ."

She wiped her nose and licked her finger. "Damn, this is some good shit."

That's how I met Mrs. Minnie. She walked me through the house, and I noticed the outlets were in the floor instead of the wall.

"Oh, baby," she said, "You didn't know this used to be a funeral home?"

I learned that years earlier, it had been a funeral home and had been converted to a house. I wanted to quit right there on the spot, but instead I went home and came back the next day with my tools to mow the grass and rake the leaves, as promised. My chores included indoor work as well: wiping the counters, washing the dishes, sweeping the floors, and taking out the garbage.

It turned out that Mrs. Minnie was well-known all over Cleveland for the parties that she gave for celebrities. I worked there for a few months, made a lot of money, and really enjoyed her company. She and I became very close.

One day, I was cleaning her house and found money all over the place, mounds of money from the night before. "What do you do with all of this money, Mrs. Minnie?" I asked her.

"Oh, baby, they were shooting dice and playing cards all night. When you're done, grab a hundred dollars off the top. That's your pay for today."

It was crazy. I cleaned her house after each party so that it was ready for the next day. After a few months, the older guys in the neighborhood caught on to my hustle and started asking Mrs. Minnie for some work. She turned them down often, and I guess that pissed them off. Hell, I was mad about them trying to take my hustle away.

One day, I went by to get my money, but she didn't answer the door. This wasn't like her, so I went home and told my father about it.

"I hope she's not trying to duck you," he said. "Give her a little while. She'll answer."

I waited a bit longer and tried again. Still no answer. So I walked around her house to the side window where her bedroom was, figuring that she was probably just tired from the night before and must've been asleep. I tiptoed so as not to alarm anyone, but the old leaves crunched beneath my feet. I took another step, keeping quiet the whole time. I didn't want to startle Mrs. Minnie if she was there. She was known to shoot out of her house every now and then, and I didn't want to get shot. I jumped up a few times to look in the window, which was about six feet off the ground, but I couldn't see anything. Then I grabbed the bricks right below the window. Struggling to pull myself up, I got a good grip and swung my legs upward to get a better grip on the other bricks. I rested for a moment to catch my breath, balancing on the bricks at the bottom of the window.

After a few moments, I slowly lifted my head up, easing my eyes into the window, in a peekaboo way. She was there, all right—in her bed, dead, with a broomstick sticking out of her buttocks. Someone had killed her.

What a sad day for me. She was a great person to know and to work for. I missed her dearly from that day forward.

CHAPTER 33

Lost and Turned Out

Cocaine and steak

I've always had an insatiable appetite for dark-skinned women. Lisa, the one who was twenty-one when I was fifteen, was dark-skinned, and so it began there. But my dark-skin demons hadn't really reared their ugly heads yet. That happened to me while I was in the tenth grade, eating lunch in the cafeteria. There were two cafeterias in my school, and for some reason, this one was the more ghetto of the two. Most of the tough, mean, sneaky, ill-mannered young students ate there. It was also more fun there, wild as hell. They had a different selection of food, more noise, and we were able to get away with acting a fool. The women behind the counter serving food were older than we were, and they would even flirt with us while serving our food.

As I sat in my seat this one day, a young lady swaying across the cafeteria caught my eye. She had wide hips and a big booty. This intimidated me. I had never seen a young lady in the ninth grade with a body like that. I was excited and terrified, but she had no clue.

As I mentioned before, while attending Shaw High School,

if you had nice clothes, shoes, jewelry, or money, or if you were an athlete, you could be popular and in with any crowd. I was blessed to have several things: a little money and nice clothes, including shoes, but what topped if off was my hair. I had my mother's hair, so it was quite wavy. If you had some nice waves, the girls really liked that, and most of the girls at my school loved my hair.

The women at my high school were very mature at an early age. Most of them smoked cigarettes and weed, and back then, that was attractive—at least to me. They'd come to school high on most days, then go across the street to the nearest gas station and buy all kinds of candy, food, juice, and chewing gum. You could tell which ones were high because they'd laugh all the time, chew gum, wear sunglasses, and smell of perfume—not to mention, they looked nice. Our school was loaded with nice-looking girls.

The girl of mention this day was dark, very confident, smoked cigarettes and weed, and from what I was told, her father had money. Little did I know, my first conversation with her would change my life.

As I sat there minding my own business, she came up and said, "Your hair looks nice. Can I rub it?"

Of course she could, and that was the beginning of me being turned out by a dark-skinned girl. We'll just call her Delores. Delores had a lot going for her. She was built well, had money, made great conversation, her hair was always done, and she had a nose ring and little plump lips. Her skin was smooth, she wore nice clothes, and she kept her nails done.

My first instinct was to get the hell out of the cafeteria. I was terrified of her, intimidated, nervous, and afraid that concentrating in class would be impossible. Instead, I stayed. We talked for a while, laughed, joked, and she rubbed my hair. I looked at her ass, smiled in her face, and just sat there in amazement. What did she want with me? I was sixteen, and she was older. I was only a tenth-grader and didn't really have much to offer her.

Lunch ended and the day went by. I saw her a couple more times in passing. We flirted, and I hurried to get to class. I felt my demons coming out every time I saw her. I knew then that this was going to be a whirlwind of an event. Even though I was already experienced with older women, and I'd already had my penis sucked, I wasn't ready for Delores. As the week went on, I avoided her.

My friends in class kept telling me, "Hey, man, this dark-skinned chick is looking for you."

I was scared as hell, so I rejected her the first few times.

I heard all of the rumors about her, but they were good rumors. She was dating a senior at our school. He was a well-known dude who ran track and dressed really nice. Why me? I guess I looked innocent, a nice-looking young man who had a job, but I was still no match for her boyfriend. He was a senior, and that meant a lot to me. He was taller, older, and more established—very popular, as well.

Still, as the weeks went by, somehow I built up the confidence to speak to Delores. My first mistake. We spoke on our way home on the bus after school, and as we got closer to her stop, I felt an incredible emotion come over me. Not only were we flirting, but I was getting horny. With the fear of my father resting in the back of my mind, I was thinking of going over to this girl's house after school, knowing damn well I should've been going home.

My father had changed his working hours at this point, so there were no more late-night extravaganzas for us. He now worked from seven a.m. to three p.m., and he was home when my sister and I got home from school. He made a work list for us, and everything had better be done. My sister and I became great at doing what he asked, because if we didn't, even if we merely forgot, we got our asses beat. I didn't want any part of that. My father was big and strong, and he didn't play. Still, my sex demons started to take over while on the bus.

As we approached Delores's stop, she got up and said, "Why don't you come over for a little while?"

I jumped at the chance to be with her after school. Even though I knew my father had a work list, I didn't care, and my sex demons were in rare form. As we walked down her street, a car came by, but she just waved, and we kept on walking. She told me that was her grandmother, headed off to work. I then knew what was up for sure. We were going to engage in something: sex, smoking (for her), or just chilling. We got into her house and it was immaculate, with red carpet, white leather furniture, a chandelier hanging from the ceiling, beautiful art pieces, and a host of other nice things. We entered, closed the door, walked to the couch, and sat down.

I was wrong about the chill part. She did smoke, but what happened next put my sex demons in rare form. She sent me down to her basement, where I waited for about fifteen minutes. When she finally came downstairs, she had a demonic look in her eyes. I was terrified, horny, spooked, and worried all at once. I smelled weed, chewing gum, and that perfume again— and all of it made my fear, worry, and confusion melt away.

Delores was very energetic, aggressive, and super turned on. I was sixteen and going crazy, while she was much more experienced, high, and in rare form. She snatched my clothes off without asking me, my mind racing and going back to my babysitter days. I was ready, but in the back of my mind, I was thinking about my father being home and his work list. It was crazy, but amazing at the same time.

As she took my clothes off, she was breathing harder and harder, and so was I. We were sweating, kissing, rubbing, and all of a sudden, she grabbed my crotch—grabbed it mercilessly. I immediately reset back to what Marco did. I was confused because she grabbed me like that man had grabbed me, but in front of me was this dark chocolate woman, high on weed, aggressive, and kissing me. That was when Delores went down on me. I'd had this before, but nothing like this. It was amazing. I was sixteen, at this girl's house, and she had a boyfriend.

Delores was extremely high, so her aggression, at times, got the best of me. I was almost in tears as she bit my arms, chest (which felt good), and then my neck. She bit my neck as if she were a carnivore. She drew blood, and when she did, she became even more demonic. I wore the scars from her teeth marks on my neck for months. I guess she was marking her territory. Even my friends at school noticed the marks. They were not passion marks. They were marks of a woman high on weed and cocaine, super turned on, and unstoppable. As she bit my neck, my toes curled in pain and not passion, but there was nothing I could do. I was in the room with another monster, but I enjoyed this monster.

We finished having sex, took a break, and Delores asked me to come upstairs.

She opened the refrigerator and said, "Pick a steak of your choice."

I chose a huge, thick, juicy T-bone steak, and she cooked it for me there on the spot. This huge, king-size steak—man, I was in heaven. By this time, it was about ten p.m. and now I was definitely in trouble. We ate, talked, and laughed, and then Delores told me to reach behind myself and hand her a bag. I did so, and to my amazement, she took out a bag of cocaine, poured out a line, snorted it, and went back down on me. I was done. A steak, sex, oral, and a good-looking lady high on weed and cocaine just taking advantage of me.

I left Delores's house around eleven that night. This dark-skinned woman turned me out. I had rejected her weeks ago, so I owed her a pound of flesh, and she more than took it.

I got home around eleven-thirty p.m. My father went off, but I didn't care because he had no clue what I had just gone through. I was lost and turned out. Delores turned me out, and like Rick James said, cocaine is a helluva drug. Still, this wasn't all fun and games. Using drugs at such an early age can and will have devastating effects on the mind and body. You'll develop a tendency to chase that first high over and over again. You'll never get it again, though, no matter how much you try to keep using that drug or try using different ones. In most cases, the early drug users I've known eventually turned to crack or heroin. As for Delores, it later ruined her life.

CHAPTER 34

Of Sound Mind, Body, and Soul

**Two of my best jobs
General Electric/Angela Mia Pizza,
I worked at the pizza place under age,
and got fired, but I loved it**

THIS ISN'T WHERE the story ends for me. Here's what came next.

I was in an auto mechanics class at Shaw High School. It was an easy class, and it wound up being pretty fun. One day, my senior counselor asked our mechanics teacher if he could talk to me. I was ordered to his office, and so I went. I was a little nervous when I sat down and the counselor started talking.

"Mr. Walker," he said, "are you interested in working for General Electric?"

I thought for a minute, and then answered yes. I had no clue what I was doing, no electrical skills, nothing. I just knew how to make pizzas because up until that point I had been working at a pizza shop. I told my counselor that.

He laughed. "Well, first you have to get through the interview next week. Be ready. Now get back to class."

Next week came soon enough, and I headed up to General Electric. *This place is huge*, I thought to myself.

It was at the top of Noble Road in East Cleveland, spread out on a lot of acres, and I was intimidated. As I walked in, a nice white lady handed me a name tag and asked me to have a seat. I sat there, palms sweaty, looking around, noticing how nice everything was.

Just then the door swung open and a tall man with bushy hair popped out. "Mr. Walker, how are you?"

I greeted him back, we shook hands, and he invited me in. Before the interview, I had studied a bit at home, looking up General Electric and learning about the company so that I could kill the interview.

He asked his first question: "What can you do for General Electric?"

With me being a quick thinker, and the fact that I had studied their company, I had an answer right away. "Sir," I said, "I can bring energy, motivation, a good attitude, and I like to help people."

He looked at me with a huge smile on his face, as if he was impressed with my answer. I guess so, because I got the job, and there were four other people in there for the same job. I worked at General Electric for about a year. It was a great time and great pay, too. My job was to unpack little meters, test them, put a metal plate on top of them, repack them, and put them outside of the office for shipping—very easy and cool.

This is the approach I've taken toward every job I've had in life to this day: huge smile, motivation, energy, helping, giving back, being polite, and having respect for everyone. I am the same person today.

In my senior year of high school, I was working at GE,

and then one day in 1982, heading into 1983, I heard an announcement over the school PA system.

"If you would like to take the ASVAB test today, report to the cafeteria. I repeat, if you would like to take the ASVAB today, report to the cafeteria."

All of us who had signed up the previous month were to take an exam for the Armed Services that day, so we made our way to the cafeteria immediately. Like most high school seniors, I had no idea what I was going to do with my life. I was scared, nervous, and unsure. All sorts of things were going through my mind.

I walked into the cafeteria and came face-to-face with a whole bunch of recruiters. I had an interest in the military because of my family lineage. My grandfather was in the Air National Guard, my father was in the army, and his brothers were in the army as well—both of my uncles. One of my uncles fought in the Korean War. He'd always tell us about his days in the war—pretty good stories, too. In addition, my father would always talk about his days in the army when he played running back on their football team. I loved hearing those stories.

From the outset, because of my uncles, my goal was to join the army, but that quickly changed. My brother had become a marine. He was the honor man in boot camp, to be exact, so those were my two choices.

I sat down to take the test. It took about three hours, and I didn't feel great about it at all. I went in to take the test just to get out of art class. To me it was a three-hour break, so I put no effort into it.

Back to class I went. A few of us talked about the questions and how long the test was, but I didn't care. I wanted to go into the military but wasn't confident enough to do well on the test, nor did I have any plans for life. I had no clue what I wanted to do. I didn't take the ACT or the SAT, wasn't prepared for college, hadn't taken any type of math class since the eighth grade. I truly wasn't prepared for life after high school. Every time the colleges would come to our school for some sort of orientation, I would just leave school and go to General Electric early.

Not only did I not plan to go to college, but I was embarrassed to take any test, and this stayed with me for years. Maybe I would have felt differently if I had put more effort into school, but I hadn't, and I was terrified of going to college. At this point in my life, there wasn't a person in my family with a college degree. It wasn't our culture. My family members were just workers: both sets of grandparents, my parents, uncles, aunts, all of them. They never spoke about college, just sports, mechanics, work, and women. That was my way of thinking as well. What was I going to do?

A few weeks later, the test scores came back. My senior counselor called me into his office because there were kids lined up to see recruiters, and once the scores come out, the recruiters were like hawks on meat. The recruiters reviewed the scores and immediately rushed up to the school.

Shaw High School was known to produce great test scores, not only SAT scores, but the Armed Services Vocational Aptitude and Battery (ASVAB) scores as well. That day in school, I saw a bunch of men in uniform. I peeked around the corner, not sure of how bad I had done. Shame engulfed me.

Lots of people were in the lunchroom—kids lined up, people smiling—yelling out their high scores, so I figured, *Hell, he called me into the office to talk to a recruiter. Maybe I passed after all.*

There were two lines: a line for those who passed, and a line for those who failed. I stood there confused and scared, nervous about the results. The counselor saw me looking lost, and with a strong, swift swing of his arm, he pointed me in the direction of one of the lines. He was always grumpy, with a shitty look on his face, so I didn't know what the line meant, pass or fail. It was a short line, with maybe three people in it, so we stood out. I had that real gut feeling, a bad one. Life had been going pretty well for me, but a feeling of being a failure consumed me once again. As I walked past the recruiters, not one of them looked at me. They knew the failure line quite well. I felt horrible, but I still wasn't sure which line was passing and which one was the failure line.

I thought that I would surely get snatched up by one of the recruiters and asked to join the military. As I walked by them, I entered the counselor's office, and he handed me my score. Once I made eye contact with him again, I knew. He had a look of disgust on his face as if I had failed, and I had. It was one of the most embarrassing situations I had ever experienced in my life. I had to walk back out of his office and pass those who passed the test. Everyone knew: the counselor, the students, and the recruiters. It was like being a dumb kid that no one wanted to be around.

One of my so-called friends said, "Doubleo, what did you score? I scored an 88." He waved his scores around, bragging.

What he did started something burning inside me. It grew and grew and grew. He was known to be a smart kid. We all knew that. But he was fat, and so I said to him, "Your fat ass can't go into the military anyway." I was still pissed about his bragging. Everybody knew that I had failed that test, but nobody knew how badly I had failed. I kept it a secret until June 6, 2016, 9:45 a.m., when I started writing my book. I scored 11, a measly 11 out of 99.

That wasn't my last chance, though. Later in the school year, the recruiters were going to come back to our school to administer the ASVAB again. I was terrified, not sure about this test, either. The last thing I wanted was to be embarrassed again. I didn't want to fail the exam, but I had to do something with my life. I had to put myself on the line. No recruiters were calling, no college coaches were calling. Most of my friends had taken the SAT and passed. Most of my friends had a plan for life after high school. A lot of them had passed the ASVAB, had a recruiter, and were on their way to the military. But not me. I had nothing.

I decided to study just a little and to apply myself a little more. I practiced a few definitions, worked some math problems, practiced mechanical inclination problems, studied paragraph comprehension, etc. I felt just a little better about the ASVAB, and I now had a clue about what I had seen on the test before. I had confidence. I just needed to score higher.

Eventually the announcement came again over the PA: "All students wishing to take the ASVAB, please report to the cafeteria."

I hesitated, nervous and intimidated, but I knew what I had to do. I headed to the cafeteria and spoke to the counselor.

He looked at me, smirking, as if to say, "Not you, again."

I just looked straight ahead. We got the test, I grabbed my pencil, and the test started. I still didn't understand much of what was on the test. The math was out of my league, and I had this horrible feeling of failure running through me. The test ended, I went back to class, and then I left school for work at General Electric by noon.

Days went by, weeks went by, and after a month or so, I was back in school when the senior counselor called me into his office.

"Have a seat, young man," he said, and he didn't look happy.

I knew that the next thing out of his mouth would be bad news, and indeed it was.

"You failed the test again. Are you stupid?"

I was hurt. I couldn't believe he'd said that to me. At this point, I had a clue that I wanted to go to the military, but I still had not prepared enough. We were close to graduating, I had failed the test for a second time, and I could not afford to go to college. Even if I could have, I hadn't taken the SAT. I was so hurt, devastated, and scared that I cried. I asked the counselor what my score was.

He smirked and said, "You scored a 30."

A 30? How could I be so stupid? But I scored 19 points more than I did the last time. In my mind, it was an improvement.

What did I do to improve? It wasn't a lot, but I did improve. What helped me was my mind-set. Now I was absolutely determined to go into the military, and now I had a plan. I had goals and could see them clearly. There was something that I wanted, so I went after it. I knew what I had to do to reach my goal, and really, it was a simple recipe. Study harder, study longer, and apply myself. You see, I would take the test a third time. I wanted it, I needed it, and that was also the difference. I knew the answer. I had found my purpose.

Purpose fuels passion.

CHAPTER 35
It Clicked and I Felt It

This is when my life changed forever

Arrogance has no place

Don't see things as they are.
See them as they can be.

VISUALIZE WHO YOU want to be and aim for that person, inside and out. I now had just enough confidence. It wasn't only the confidence that propelled me. It was coupled with something much stronger and more intense than that. It pierced my soul. I heard and felt the *click*. Just so you know, when it clicks, you'll feel it all over your body. It's an amazing feeling, and you will feel it from the bottom of your feet to the top of your head. Once it clicked, I knew that I was on to something. With the fact that I now knew how to get, gain, and maintain the level of confidence that I now had, I had found the answer, and it was a thing of beauty.

For many years, I felt dumb, stupid, and sometimes even left out. My failing of the ASVAB twice put me in a position to think and to use the brain that I never knew how to use. I was fueled by failure and pushed by anger.

There is extreme motivation in anger, and I had that. I was angry about my family's divorce. I was angry about losing our house. I was angry about pissing in bed. I was angry about being molested. I was angry about being groped. I was angry about not having any food, lights, water, or heat. I was angry about my mother leaving us. I was angry about going to court and possibly heading to a foster family. I was angry about failing the ASVAB and not having a future. For years, I never did anything about any of it. And then I finally did something with my anger. I channeled it, put it in perspective, bottled it up, and directed it at anything and everything that I wanted to accomplish.

My counselor looking at me with that stupid smirk on his face after he gave me my score when I failed the second time didn't bother me. He had no clue that I had just figured out why I had improved. I looked right back at him with that same grin.

"Are you angry?" he asked.

"Nope," I said. "As a matter of fact, I'm extremely pleased."

"But you failed . . . again."

"No," I said, "I didn't. I learned, and I passed. I passed the mental block that I've had for many years."

A recruiter heard us talking and asked, "What's wrong? You failed the test."

Again I repeated, "But I passed. I got past the mental block that I've had for years." I then asked him what score I would need in order to get into the military.

"A 31," he told me. Then he looked at that dreadful sheet with all of those scores on it, and he said, "You got a 30. Well, what are you going to do?"

Without missing a beat, I said, "Man, I'm taking that bitch again."

Conclusion

If you don't do something,
something will do you.

CHAPTER 36

No Life—Figure It Out

Extraordinary people are ordinary people with extra.
What was your defining moment? When did it click?

S O THIS IS the story of the first half of my life: growing up
in East Cleveland, surrounded by more trauma and pain
than most people ever experience in a lifetime. There is so
much more to my story, but not enough space to tell it all here:
the story of how I became a father and a husband. For now,
though, it's time to wrap up the story of this young and broken
boy they called Doubleo.

There was another character in this story, one who was
always with me, but I didn't realize it until later. Many times,

many days, and many years, I either skipped out on church or attended infrequently. When I was a kid, we went to church, but it wasn't to pay praise to God. We went for the milk and cookies that they served. Out of all those years of attending church, I had no clue what it was about, nor did I pay attention. I did know, however, that I was a child of God. Neither here nor there, I knew I was covered. Being a child of God, you're a child, so you don't know how to receive his message—at least I didn't. Receiving his blessings became more profound for me as I got older. And that was when I realized that God had been waiting for me all along.

It took a long time. It didn't all set in until I had reached almost fifty years of age. I honestly now feel that I may not be on this earth too much longer. I'm not sure why I feel that way, how my death will happen, or what lies ahead for me, but I do know that there is something truly more worthy awaiting me. However, I may be here much longer than I believe, and if I am, this journey that I'm on will have been well worth it. I didn't ask for this to happen, whatever it is, but it's so embracing it has become a way of life for me and has seemed quite natural.

If something happens to you, regardless of what it is, someone will say, "Everything happens for a reason," but no one will ever tell you what that reason was. It's up to you to find out, to conduct some deep soul-searching, rethink your day, retrace your tracks, your passage, your everything. It's worth it to find that reason. The reason may shock you and lead you on into deeper things, thoughts, successes, and a new you. We all have a new you in us each and every day. It's there every morning you wake up and can affect your family for the next four generations, both good and bad. It depends on what you do with the new you.

Based on my readings, specifically a book entitled *Switch On Your Brain* by Dr. Caroline Leaf, I've learned quite a few things.

Mainly, I've learned that how we think not only affects our own spirit, soul, and body, but it also impacts the people around us. This isn't new to me, but for years I didn't use the process of science and scripture. They both show how the results of our decisions pass through the sperm and ova and into those next generations that I mentioned, profoundly affecting their choices and lifestyles.

Dr. Leaf writes, "After God, your mind is the next most powerful thing in the universe."

Regardless of what I pass to my children, I am now more educated on how the things I pass to them can and will affect them, and what's good about the passing of my genes. I know the bad, I feel the good, and I'm extremely aware of how to manage the effects of it all.

While everything happens for a reason, the truth of the matter is that most of us do not want to know that reason, simply because we can't deal with or cope with reality. Quite frankly, most of us don't want to know the truth, and that's why people fail at growing. Those who do not want to deal with or cope with reality would rather remain stuck in suspended animation. It becomes a game of sorts, a game with themselves that leads them into society thinking the same way, affecting the workplace, family, and friends. In the military, having this train of thought can get people killed, causing units to fail, ships to collide, and lives to be destroyed—all because of refusal to accept reality, even though it's only reality that will ultimately result in becoming a better person. I did this, as well, but fortunately no lives were at stake under my leadership. No one died, nor did any ships collide. Had I not been surrounded by mature, solid, and caring people, my mistakes could have been grave.

We lie, cheat, and deceive to make those around us feel better about us or better about being around us. Eventually, though, the real you will always come out. Depending on how many people you have deceived in the past, the real you will come out at the most inopportune time. Specifically, at a job interview, applying for a loan, during your marriage . . . it will manifest itself, and there will be nothing you can do about it. It may not directly impact you at the time, but it may transform itself through your kids, your parents, or a very close friend. You never know.

What I am saying is this: invest in yourself so that you may, as a human being, invest righteously in others. Become interested in yourself. That's a selfless act if done correctly, as it not only works for you, but also works in favor of those around you. It gives pleasure, and makes your aura genuine and noticeable.

Don't get me wrong. I'm not perfect by any stretch of the imagination. Nor have I practiced what I'm saying over the years, but having passed the age of fifty, I'm doing so now. I've been able to, over the years, speak with hundreds and even thousands of people quite candidly for the most part. Most times, I had to also believe in what I was telling them because as I know now, it was given to me by God. I was chosen as his messenger to those I talked to. I know this to be true because I've watched them flourish from what I've told them. That was my gift, but I never capitalized on it until later on in my life. I didn't cherish my gift. Therefore, it wasn't doing me any good. Others, yes, but not me personally. This was what I thought until I finally figured out that I was giving back. Giving back was my gift to give, and I did this without reservation.

We all have an innate ability to pierce someone's soul with encouraging words, good thoughts, a warm gesture, or even a simple hello. However, based on the deadly sins—jealousy, for one—we become reserved in our quest to help others, or we refuse to see people do better than we're doing. Although I've never been jealous of anyone, my ways were the devil's ways.

There was a time in my life that I didn't believe in God. I truly believed in the devil. He gave me all of the good things that were bad for me. I made myself believe that they were good so that I didn't have any guilt. The devil gave me everything that I craved. He had many faces, so many that at one time, I believed he had more faces than God. The world's hell—sin, corruption—was what felt like heaven to me. I thought I was having fun, but I was really falling into the depths of sin and dying inside all along.

Most times in my young life, I was merely going through the motions. That was when I knew that the things I was doing were wrong. Even then, it still took me years to overcome the craving, temptation, greed, and lust. I chose the lies of Satan and spiraled into mental, physical, and spiritual disarray. I've always believed in myself regardless of the stronghold the devil had on me, though.

The devil broke the wrong parts of me.
He broke my wings, and forgot that I had claws.
I am on a journey to heaven.
I no longer love the devil's ways.

Life is given to us, and it's not taken away by our creator, but taken away by sinful people. If your life is ever taken by someone else, they've just enabled you to achieve the highest honor any human being could imagine: heaven. If you don't believe in heaven, you'll stay in hell.

I had to begin my journey. I get my guidance and direction from God. Below are a few things that I go by daily.

H.A.B.I.T.—Have a Better Idea Today: I infuse this approach into my life every day. Regardless of what you are doing, it can be the foundation for your success. I'm not saying it's easy, but if you make it a habit, it becomes the norm for you, just like breathing. You can't afford not to breathe, so therefore, you cannot afford not to have a better idea each day. Even if you keep your idea to yourself, allow it to grow inside of you. Give it a chance. Becoming the person you are meant to become is only hard when you realize that you are on your sublime journey. It's supposed to be hard, tough, and irritating. You will experience all of those things if you approach it with zeal and obedience.

Wandering through life aimlessly is extremely easy. You have nothing to do, nothing to be responsible for, no worries, and no challenges. You are simply adrift. When you see two people in a relationship, unhealthy, living day to day, borrowing money, late with their bills, raising rude children, just living basic, those are the people I am referring to. There's a continued infusion of unhealthy people into this world because of the people before them: their parents. Don't ever be content with where you are currently. You have so much more to give and so much more to offer. Power isn't given to us. It's earned.

Even then, it's not called power. It's called "application." Go deep into your soul to find that gift. Find it, then apply it. It will not come easy. Most of us use it every day, but don't realize it. Applying what you have as a gift is the process of application. Take a step back, first and foremost, and ask yourself, "What is my reason to live?" Search for it. Feel it deeply. When you find it, you will know. You will experience a sensation like a soothing force of lightning that runs through your body with a sense of euphoria. Notice the feeling, and then capture that moment with your soul. Keep it and remember it, and then make it your reason to live. Live through it. Apply it and think it into existence.

For most of us, our reason for living is for our kids, our family, or someone we love. However, that's not good enough. Your reason to live must be something that has eternal staying power. Our kids grow up, move away, and leave an emptiness when they go. That's why I mention that staying alive for your kids isn't a good enough reason. If you're only living for them and they leave, what do you have to fall back on that will keep you loving yourself, loving life? Family members may become distant, move on, move away, or die. When that happens, if you've made them the reason that you live, what will you do?

If you're the type of person who wants power, you can achieve that. However, if you do it right—either at work, with your family, or with friends—at the end of your day, you should feel powerless. Feeling powerless when giving is what you should aspire to achieve. Only the real people will either attain this or want to. Those who feel weak or drained at the end have done it for the wrong reason, and are not meant to be any type of messenger. Their thoughts were in the wrong place. Their plans were either evil or not meant for the right reason, and their thoughts carried ill intent. Application happens every day, but if done incorrectly or not from the heart, people believe that either they made a mistake somewhere or it was the other person's fault. They might even believe that the act of application—having power—doesn't exist, and then they will quit.

Instead, you must make it a habit to become better every day. In life, if you fall, try to fall onto your back, because if you can look up, you can get up. Get up and stay up, but remember how you fell. Falling down will happen often in your life. Embrace it so that you're ready, or at least prepared for it, next time. Every time you fall, you *must* get up and become stronger and stronger. Some examples of falling are breaking up a relationship, divorcing, losing a game, failing a test, lying, cheating, etc. Know your successes, but know your failures, too. That's how you know when to get up.

Do these things as I have, and you will find happiness. My

life and your life will change every day. My prior life was good, but what's ahead for me will be great. I am at the pinnacle of realness, and I can feel the presence of eternal life, even here on earth.

I.D.E.A.—Implement Drive Encourage Association: you can't do everything by yourself. Again, the application of thought comes into play. A thought, an idea, that's all this world is built on. Not everyone can have these beautiful thoughts, regardless of what they are. However, we can all play our part. It can be something as simple as throwing a party for your children, painting a room, organizing a family night, or doing a host of things. In order to make this application of thought work, you have to be at a minimum a caring, passionate person. As a parent, spouse, or sibling, whoever you are charged to be, you must either have a high emotional IQ, or learn how to achieve that level of emotional intelligence. Leaders and those with a high emotional IQ have courage, empathy, passion, and are compassionate. They have huge hearts, give often, desire to see others succeed, possess high morale, and are more often than not successful.

In addition, they have a great work/life balance. You should want to see people grow. Not all people want to see people grow, and those people are full of sin. Give people ideas and watch them move forward. Doing so, you will receive great gratitude and satisfaction. Your health will blossom, as well. Some people are addicted to being upset, mean, nasty, or even full of poison and hate. They know better, but have been consumed so much with ill will, depression, and evil that they have simply become comfortable and will not be able to enjoy a better life until they apply better thoughts.

Now that I am older, I've spent many years thinking about what happened to me. I've gone through quite a few relationships, including a divorce, and I have learned many things: how precious life is, how delicate the mind really is, how the brain is the processor of your actions and thoughts, good or bad. I do not want my kids to ever experience what I went through. It has been extremely devastating, even more so because I blocked it out. Blocking it out didn't allow me to face it, learn from it, or fix it. By blocking it out, I never gave myself a fair chance to think about the events themselves or the course that my life took as a result. I am more open to taking corrective actions now, more so than I have ever been before.

Because of the traumas that I endured as a child, I lost the nice, humble, understanding person that I was supposed to become. Instead, evil thoughts, poor decisions, and above all, a wrecked human being manifested into my soul and body. It projected me into a cruel world without a strong moral foundation.

I work hard to correct these things now. I'm an avid reader of and about life, about inner peace, actions, and reactions. I pay more attention to others' feelings. Not only do I respect myself more, but I have earned the respect of others. I care deeply, not only for family and friends, but also for people with whom I'm less familiar. I understand now how my words and actions can help, hurt, or even move a person to tears, happiness, or at worst, extreme sadness.

No, I didn't get this right on my first, second, or third try. But as I was behaving badly, it began to hurt me to see my children, friends, or loved ones hurting because of me. In other words, I developed a conscience. My morals and standards got much better and clearer, and I now had a reason to live. Everything turned around when I started wanting to be a better example: not wanting to let my kids down or fail my friends and family, and most of all, not wanting to fail God.

I wish I had done something sooner to process the traumas of my early life. As long as I continued to hide these stories, holding them in and pretending that they never happened, I didn't heal. More than anyone, my daughter has suffered for this. She didn't have the father that she should have had like my sons did. I have deep regret for that, and I have to live with the fact that we will never get that time back.

However, today, I am a better person and father simply because of my wrongdoings. Even though I have a lot of lost time with regard to my daughter, the lost time keeps me searching for new time, better times, and for a way to be more present. For many years, I wasn't a good person, nor was I a good father. My father had always been a great man. During the divorce proceedings of my parents, his parenting was reduced, but he was still a great provider. I did the same thing after my divorce, providing from a distance. My mother divorcing him played a major part in my father being away from us, and I suffered from it. My kids experienced a lack in parenting on my behalf, almost the exact same way things had gone with my own father. I was the wrongdoer in my marriage. If I could do it all over, I would, realizing that marriage, a great marriage, takes time—not work, but time. The consequences that the kids suffer are almost never-ending.

Only now am I learning to cleanse my soul, my spirit, and my being. I am more aware now than at any other point in my life. Now, I am always in my purpose. I want my kids to learn from my mistakes and to know what my upbringing was like. I want them to be aware that they have my DNA in them, and that there is a possibility that they may repeat my actions. I want them to continue to know me—know who I was, and know who I am now. I want them to know where I came from, where I have been, and more importantly, where I am going with them.

I enjoy sharing my story because although I did not choose this life, over time I have grown into it. I didn't ask for it. I was a product of an environment that I did nothing about—but I could have. I share my story because I want to help those who are currently facing similar challenges. When I was young, I walked my path without a care in the world, not recognizing that I was on the path to inevitable destruction. If you are on that path and you remain there, you, too, will find destruction at the end. It's happening to you right now. It's in the growing stages, malignant at best. Do not look for a cure, but seek to be fruitful and righteous, wanting to do better, and being honest in your attempt to get there.

I want my kids to know that if they ever encounter what I've encountered—dysfunction, mistreatment, abuse—that they must repair their past in order to enjoy their present and future. The first step in this process is to become aware of it. Humbly accept your past, and even though others may not forgive you, you must forgive yourself. You can also forgive those who don't forgive you. They will eventually come to understand and then appreciate your growth. I still have struggles, but I'm working on my inner self and my inner peace.

I have repented for my bad behavior, but I've done so with a purpose in mind. Repentance is the first step, but it must be followed with sincere efforts to be thoughtful, thankful, and grateful. I am now grateful for the smallest things that I took for granted for many years, the simplest things that we expect to do every day, like being able to speak and say hello, share a smile, listen, see, enjoy the world, connect with other people, witness change and growth. Even living to see another day is a blessing that I once took for granted. I have learned to always be polite, even in the most uncertain circumstances. I am a better listener.

I have become afraid of losing my life, which now makes many things much more precious to me. I was never afraid of losing my life before, and I had never thought about leaving anyone behind, but now those things matter to me. Not that they didn't before, but it wasn't something I thought about. I was just expecting to wake up and be here, existing another day on this earth. Now I *want* to be here, and I know that I have a purpose. I want to live and to help others live and to realize that they, too, have a purpose.

I am on the second part of my life now, and I have faith that this phase will be much better than the former one. There is a lot behind me. The trail I've walked will always be there, but I can tell you one thing: I am never going back. I may look back just as a reminder—a reminder that there are still other people now walking the same trail—but I will never go back. I look back sometimes to retrieve things that I can bring with me, especially others who are lost on the same trail. I am on this earth for people—who, or how many, I have no idea, but it doesn't matter. I have found my purpose on this earth, and it's connected to people.

God didn't give me a color, he didn't give me a certain race, he didn't give me a certain age. He gave me people, and I am very passionate about it. I didn't ask for this. I believe it was presented to me, and I accept it just like I've accepted all of the wrongdoing. The same way that I was *off* my trail with wrongdoing, I am *on* my trail for right going. I am going higher and higher, and it won't stop. I can't stop it. I feel it all over. Living with my spiritual and material existence in sync like this, I feel like I have finally achieved peace.

I have a special message for some of my readers. Those of you, male or female, who have suffered sexual abuse: I know what you've gone through. I know what you're thinking. I've been there. And most importantly, I know for sure that you can make it through, simply because I have. Yes, it was hard, but you can do it. If you have been raped, molested, or something else, know that others have endured similar tragedies. I was once where you are. Although it was a rough, long, tiring road, I made it through, and you can, too.

Whether you're a man or a woman, understand that you are not the first or the only one to go through these trials. You may want sex, and you may want a companion, but mentally you may shut down at times because of your extremely volatile and painful past. You have to clear and free your mind, accept what has happened, push the anger out, and seek a better mental state. During your time of healing and cleansing, what you have gone through remains, but you have to pay more attention to what you want better for yourself, your kids, and your family. For me, the thing that has helped me the most, and what continues to help me, is that I am now an advocate speaking about what happened. I talk about it often, and I never hold anything back. Helping is healing. I wanted to do better, I wanted to see better, and I found a better me. Do whatever you can to be the best you can; be the best you can, so you can do whatever you can.

People who wonder whether the glass is half-full
or half-empty are missing the point:
the glass is refillable.